FREEDOM

an optical illusion

Alton Harvy Sr.

FREEDOM

an optical illusion

Tate Publishing & Enterprises

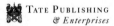

TATE PUBLISHING
& *Enterprises*

Tate Publishing is committed to excellence in the publishing industry. Our staff of highly trained professionals, including editors, graphic designers, and marketing personnel, work together to produce the very finest books available. The company reflects the philosophy established by the founders, based on Psalms 68:11,

"THE LORD GAVE THE WORD AND GREAT WAS THE COMPANY OF THOSE WHO PUBLISHED IT."

If you would like further information, please contact us:

1.888.361.9473 | www.tatepublishing.com

TATE PUBLISHING & *Enterprises*, LLC | 127 E. Trade Center Terrace Mustang, Oklahoma 73064 USA

Freedom, An Optical Illusion

I dedicate this book to my parents, who all are gone; my three sisters and one brother, who are gone; and the rest, three sisters and one brother, for always being there for me without always knowing what the outcome would be. Fred, Doris, Helen, and Faye. All of my ancestors, from the early 14th hundreds until now. The Jewish people whose lives have been ones of great horror, sacrifice and torture, but have given so much, and out of such a great loss they have gained greater strengths.

ACKNOWLEDGEMENTS

Thanks to God, to whom I give all credit for the structure and balance of my life, which comes from his precious love. And to my loving wife, Mary L., for supporting me in everything I do for almost forty-five years. I want to thank my three children, Alton Jr, Derrick, and our baby, Pechina S., for their support, because they didn't have a choice; and my three grandchildren, Beronsha, Deondre, and Ms. Brandi.

I thank Tate Publishing for making this happen, and I thank those who provided the materials for making these things complete.

Introduction

As I look back some fifty years now it seems not so long ago that I was a young boy growing up in the South on a farm near a small town in Georgia. The name of the town is Cuthbert. It sits on the south end of Georgia near the Florida line. The population wasn't that large, but there was a vast chasm in our society, racially, socially, and economically, just as there is today. The lines of injustice had long been drown in the sands of time, and they haven't been erased yet; personally I don't thank they ever will.

I came from two or three generations of sharecroppers—maybe more, I don't know—as did most black families during those times. Sharecropping was a system designed to have things remain as they were. After this so-called freedom was granted, a new type of enslavement was formed, just for the purpose of control.

After gaining constitutional freedom in 1865, which wasn't meant for us, anyway, the plantation owners supported by our elected officials had to devise a system by which they could continue using the same people, that was once their slaves and have them to continue farming their lands. Extracting coal from the mines, and doing many other different kinds of work, without any out of pocket expenses, just as they were doing before. This newfound freedom appeared to be fine at the beginning but like it's been said, "As much as thing change, they always remain the same." I say, "Nothing was changed; it's just changed around."

There was plenty of cropping but no sharing, at least where we were. My family was pretty big. There were twelve children born to Daddy and Mom—five boys and seven girls. My father's name was Douglas, my mother's name Kira, and my grandmother's name was Ethel. She was our mother's mother; she was the only grandparent I knew.

Of the children, two boys died at birth, and one girl died at a very early age. I never knew any of them, leaving Rose Lee, Laura Ann, Fred Douglas, Ethel Lee, Alton, Ed, Sally Doris, Helen Rose, and Lillian Faye. Our parents and grandparents were all Christians, and that was the key and the sole reason for our existing in those times. This was the beginning of learning how to live a free life, in a place where freedom wasn't available to people of my race.

Being a Christian was the best way of life for us then, and it still is today. While we were living in a society that didn't offer the same freedom, rights, liberties, and justice to its non- white citizens as it did its white citizens. Black people had to re-rout their way of thinking and teaching, in order to live through those sometimes harsh and dreadful times. The teachings we received came straight from the Holly Bible. We were taught to love "everybody," and that was the best thing that could have happened for us. That started from day one. Our daily lives were living a life that demonstrated a life of love. Our parents told us, "The best way to learn life was to love life, and when you love it, you'll live it well."

The teachings of loving parents, grandparents, and others around us who had the same concern for others and themselves is what inspired us to continue this way of life. That's been the badge we've worn from the very beginning.

This love we were given wasn't limited to just the people in our family or the people that felt the same or looked the same as us. This love was for everyone, bar-none, and that was the law in our home. It was without discussion.

I'm the middle child; there were four older than me and four younger than me. The chain of command was very much in place when I arrived, meaning when Dad and Mom weren't around, the oldest was in charge of keeping the rest of us in line—and in line we were. Being as far down the list as I was, I never got the chance to fill that roll, but as I think about it, I probably couldn't have handled it, anyway. I never took the times to let that become anything for me to worry about. This way, there were never any mix-ups in who was calling the shots. But the neat thing about this was whenever we were away from home the same applied. You know, like everybody's looking out for everybody, and it worked very well then and it could work now if we would lend ourselves to help each other, using the same formula that was used then. That formula was love.

We always treated each other with love and respect, just as if one of our parents was always around. This system was the universal way of life throughout Georgia and other parts of the South as far as blacks were concerned.

The higher rankers always treated the lower order well. We never had any problems with that because it was always with love. The thing that kept everything balanced was, yes, love. I hope the word "love" doesn't bother anyone too much, because it will appear quite a few times throughout this book.

Growing up on a farm, you have the chance to learn so much about so many things that could only be learned on a farm. Whether it was in Georgia or on a farm anywhere else, the lessons would be about the same. What you learned wasn't taught. It was just a day-to-day way of life. It could vary as to what one might learn, and that too would depend on what kind of farm you were on and what would be grown. Sure, there are different kinds of farms, but I will guarantee you that whatever the farm might produce, it's very hard work, and it can be dirty.

At one time, growing tobacco in most parts around our place was very popular, but that was before my time. Tobacco barns could be found on most of the large plantations throughout Georgia. There was one sitting on the edge of our baseball diamond. I will never forget that old barn. They all were built the same because they all held the same history, which served the same purpose. They were about three stores high, with racks going from side to side. They would hang the tobacco leaves over the racks to dry. The only other time we would use the barn would be for shelter when it would rain while we were playing ball; and if you ever played ball, you know it will rain. But there was evidence of other uses by passers-by from time to time. There were handrails all around it. Some of them still had old rusted arm bracelets, and just below the rail was a foot or leg iron attached to the building's foundation. This building had the image of a cold, dreadful and very lonely place. Even when the sun was bright, it seemed like it had a dark veil or an overlying shadow around it. There were some very bad stories told about that old barn. There were other plantations I knew with those barns, but the only thing they were good for was that the pigeons had a good roosting place in the rafters. But the evidence was very clear of the grim history those places held. I'm sure each had its own story but was equal in its sorrows.

As for us, we grew cotton and plenty of it. I thought Georgia was the only place on earth cotton would grow, and it seemed like we grew all of it. We also grew corn, both white and yellow, and peanuts, too—three different kinds of them. These were the main products we grew. Remember, we were sharecroppers, and the thought was the more we planted, the more we had to share. "Wrong" We also grew potatoes, red, white and sweet. We grew various kinds of beans, peas, greens, okra, and different kinds of melons. These were for food. Sugarcane was what we made syrup from. These were some of the things we grew.

You may ask, aren't there many things that can be learned no matter where one grows up? And I'll say yes without the slightest bit of hesitation. I do apologize if I made it seem like you would have to live on a farm in order to qualify for learning anything. I simply meant that learning began at a very early age and about so many different things, from ground preparation to planting and harvesting. There were different kinds of dirt that were better for growing different things. I could see at a very early age how such harmony kept a multiplicity surroundings working together with perfect synchronicity. This kept the order and balance in our daily lives. Everything played a specific part at a specific time. What a great opportunity to learn a lesson from nature how so many different things worked together without friction. What a picture.

One of the first things I learned was that the life of a farmer was very tough, but quite rewarding to say the least. But as I look back, I can see a very different way of life then, especially for blacks in the 1940s living in the South. It didn't matter where, and at that time it didn't seem right. Yet it wasn't so bad because that was the only way we knew.

We'd been conditioned to this way of living. This was the benefit we were given just for being born with black skin.

History Itself Simply Means "His Story," and This is Mine.

The South wasn't the only area that black Americans were made to feel inferior or forgotten, and in most places, that still hasn't changed. However, we never had to feel like we were different until we went around people that didn't look the same as us, or we looked the same as them, which wasn't that often. I still can't understand why. It was always said then, and still is today, "we are the ones that are different"; and all the while, my thinking was everyone was different. So I began to realize until you have something to compare to, you would never know anything except what you are accustomed to.

We are living in a society where freedom has always been a way of life for the most part, or that's what we've been taught. We believe the picture we see is real. Now remember, just because we believe it, that doesn't necessarily make it true.

The idea of freedom is used as a pacifier; something like giving babies a pacifier instead of a bottle formula. It's something to just keep them quiet until you finish doing whatever. But in our case, we weren't even given that. We were told to shut up.

We weren't allowed to associate with our white counterparts in any way. This alone seemed a little strange to me, but I soon realized that was the way our freedom was, and that wasn't going to change. Now please understand, it wasn't a matter of our only reason for gaining freedom would allow us to associate with a different person or with a different group of people. Association comes mainly by choice, but if it's your choice, then nothing or no one should have the right to say no. This is especially true when it comes to color or race, or any of the other things we've put in place to make things seem separate as before.

One Saturday evening at about 6:00 or 7:00 p.m., a black man was walking down the sidewalk. A white lady was walking in the opposite direction, and he was accused of looking her in the face (yes, just looking). This was a no-no in most parts of the South. Four white men got him and took him behind the mule stable; this was where the mules that were for sale were kept, like a used car lot. They whipped that man almost to death. Now I'm talking about being free in America. One might say this "man," meaning me, must be crazy. No, I'm not, but this system sure is, and this is just one of many such incidents of this kind. These things would happen quite often, and some were much worse, but life continued on until the next time. In town on Saturdays, this is where landowners would find people to work for them. There were plenty of plantation owners who didn't have people living on their land, so they had to hire workers to do their work. Sometimes when some of the white men would get drunk, they would gather in little packs, like holding a special meeting on the street corner, but everybody knew what their meetings were for. All the blacks would leave; it kind of reminded me of when the herds of deer or gazelle would leave the watering holes when the lions and tigers would approach. They just know it was time to find higher grounds. They knew something was brewing, and it wasn't good. The next day you would hear about some very terrible things that had happened. A black man would be found beaten, or even worse, they would be left by one of those drunken lynch mobs and absolutely nothing would be said or done. That's because some of them that was involved in these terrible acts, guess who they were, yep, some of the ones who should have been seeing that these things weren't being done, you know as the saying goes "Throw the rock and hide your hand."

School and church were always some happy times for us. The boys met and talked about what had happened since the last time we were there—fishing, hunting, and playing baseball. Basketball wasn't that popular around our part of town, and shooting marbles was about all we did other than work. Living on a farm could be very entertaining, and it was all in a day's work. That would help us do what had to be done and not really realize how bad the conditions around us were.

Sometimes black men would just disappear and were later found in another nearby town dead and always mutilated. But it just passed away like nothing had ever happened.

When fear has permeated the entire life of anyone they will find ways to accept things as they are. We've been told so many times that things are either good for our health or for our safety. But in my opinion, either of the two is true, but after it's said so many times we say it must be right.

For a young child to see someone being treated this way just because they was born with dark skin, made me wonder if something was wrong with being dark skinned. Every time they would speak to one of us, they would always refer to our skin color. But I learned later it wasn't our skin color; it was the shortcomings on their part. "Evil has its day of triumphs, but even then it's weaker than righteous defeated. Truth crushed to earth will rise again."

Some of the most common names we became used to dealing with were "darkies" and "shine." Most of the time, these names were for the good ones, as they say. It would be the old common name, nigger—this one was most used by all of them. I truly believe they thought it was ok. "You good for nothing, you all are lower than dogs." You all are lazy, even though we were the ones doing all of the work how could we be considered as lazy? "Shiftless, scarecrows, porch- monkeys, coons," I have no idea where any of these names came from. The condescending, and damaging low ration, never stopped. Our parents would always remind us how we must love everybody in spite of their bitterness towards us. But some of these different names are still being used today in places one might not expect it to be, but it hasn't left. All of the black men were called "boy," and when they were old, they became "uncles." The women were called "gals" and then "aunt."

There was one dear lady; her name was Mrs. Knighting. She said she would rather a rattlesnake crawl through her front door before a (nigger) come in her back door. But when she was lying on her back, suffering with something that couldn't be cured (maybe hate was eating her away) and had nobody to help her, yes, it was a black woman who took care of her. These are some of the things we had to tolerate from the very beginning. Now toleration doesn't mean its ok. It means deal with it and keep doing what you're doing and not allowing it take control of you.

I'm so glad we were taught how to love in spite of the person.

Dad said, "We were not responsible for how other people treated us, but we were responsible for how we treated others." Rev. Dr. Martin Luther King, Jr., had not begun his movement for freedom and justice yet, but he said it so eloquently, when he said, and I quote, "We must not be guilty of wrongful deeds. Let us not seek to satisfy our thirst for freedom by drinking from the cups of bitterness and hatred." End quote.

These were the teachings we received from the beginning by learning there was a better way to live, we also learned there was a better way of being free. Freedom isn't a right; freedom is a choice, and toleration doesn't mean its ok. It means that you learn to keep going and use every negative as an opportunity for something positive. You know, just ignore it, because if you don't, it will eventually consume you. These names were like our birth names, and I guess they were, because that's when they started using them—at birth. But the bad thing is, much of this still exists today in every place throughout America.

Daddy tried to keep this part of America's way of freedom for blacks away from us as much as he could. But no body tried to hide it because they all did it at sometime or another. Some of the whites were just afraid of trying to help the blacks, and the blacks had nothing to say about anything because if they did, well, it would be curtains for them.

Now I see the real benefits in knowing how to rise above the difficulties of injustice and prejudices that many in this nation are still practicing.

Daddy would take us to town about once every two months or so, and this was a big treat for us. It gave us the chance to see our friends that lived in other area around where we lived. It was quite a distance between neighbors; for the most part we would only see each other when we went to town, except for the few that went to the same school or church.

Our parents didn't go to town every week because there was always plenty of work to do, which was most important. Sometimes it would be weeks before a trip was needed, but that was all right, too. After we finished our daily work, Daddy, Mom, Momma Ethel, and the entire family would play different games. We would roast peanuts in the open fireplace, bake sweet potatoes under the hot ashes from the wood that kept us worm. We sing songs, listen to the radio, and our parents would tell us stories about how they got to the point where they were. Everyone would participate in basically everything we did, and we always had fun.

These were times the family spent with each other keeping the unity together that made the family's relationship stronger. These were the same threads that kept the unity of the black society together for so many years. When I say tighter, I mean like one big family whose needs were basically the same and the common concerns for each other was absolutely the same. Only if people had kept that same spirit I'm sure thing would be much better for everyone. Because that was the only way we could and did survive. We were completely separated from the white world, but it taught us by using the right formula and reaching out to our fellowman, we would have triumph out of tragedies.

Although we were able to keep a society of people together and quit strong, by loving and caring for each other, helping each other when help was needed and that was most of the time. Learning from the history books was one thing. But learning it first hand how the values of keeping a strong positive image within the communities, those history books didn't teach that. The real truth about black history still isn't being taught today.

This close-knit way was the energy that kept the American black families strong and ready for what awaited us the next day. It was our hangout time; this is how families found pleasure and fun with each other. Some times Daddy would put all of us into the wagon and we would go visiting some of the neighbors, who were sometimes a few miles away. Sometimes others would visit us with no invitation needed. It would always be food, conversation, and lots of encouragement to each other. The young ones would play games until time to go hide and seek, or just make up things as we went. That would go really well, but as I think about it, that's the way all the games started—just by doing it. These were very special times for us, learning to read, spell, and improving our math skills by using peanuts and/or grains of corn for our calculators. Texas instruments were still in the developing stages. But these were very good times just to enjoy the comfort of each other.

We had a system we used that worked pretty well, and it wasn't too bad considering the options and the odds.

The times when Dad and Mom didn't go to town, we had what was known as the rolling store. It would come twice a week, Tuesdays and Fridays. (Friday didn't mean it was payday. That's a day that never came; just another day in the seven-day week.) There was a truck about twenty feet long, like a moving van with shelves on each side with an aisle in the center. The driver had any and every thing on this truck that you could get in town from the stores. He was an independent home-delivery serviceman. The neat thing about it was, if there was something you wanted and didn't have the money for, which was quite often, there were two ways you could get what you needed. One was to use the swap and exchange system; you could exchange whatever you had that was of value. We learned everything has some value. We had what most people in town needed: fresh eggs two for a nickel; preserves; meats, such as smoked ham, bacon, salt pork; veggies and potatoes. These were good for the people that lived in town because they didn't have the advantage of growing their own. So we supplied their needs, and with that, our needs were met as well. Secondly, he would just trust you to pay him later. After all, where were you going?

Anything the town people needed, he had it. The more items he got from us, the farmers, the more he would have to sell for cash. Only if we were willing to share ourselves with each other now, things would be much better in every way.

We were taught about how personal possessions would not only control you, but also if you held them closely, they would be your downfall. If we couldn't share it with others, we didn't need it for ourselves. The things you held tightly would soon bring you down.

Everything was separate. Signs were posted everywhere you went, reading "whites only" and "colored." All public places, water fountains, movie theaters, the bus station, and public parks there were two parks. One we were not allowed to visit at no time, and the other one we could visit only when the white patrons weren't visiting. If they came while we were there, and yes they would come just to see us run. Yes, we would leave and of course without hesitation.

At the movie, the whites sat on the lower level, and the blacks sat in the balcony. Now you tell me how much sense this made. "Can you see something coming?"

"Yes."

We would throw popcorn and the boxes down on them, and of course it wouldn't be where we were sitting. We wondered why the seating arrangement wasn't reversed. Sometimes, even in the South, we had a slight edge. That alone told me that this just wasn't right. This was giving me a true picture of this thing called freedom. This was the best time to learn what Daddy and Mom were teaching us—how to live free, no matter what the conditions around you may be. I think they must have known as long as we were living in America, we would never be free. So they were preparing us how to live free, regardless of what the situation might be, and I might add there were plenty of those situations waiting.

THE ONE MAN RACE

If a man is running a race alone, he can lose the race if he quits running. Although we were kept from being free, they couldn't stop us from living free. Like the man running the race, if we kept running, we would cross the finish line. Only when you quit running is the race over, and we were taught to never quit, nor be controlled by the surroundings or the conditions. We had to just keep living free. Don't stop giving, loving, caring, and sharing. We were told no matter how little we might have, we always had enough to share with others. If any were in need, all were in need.

Most conditions are temporary, anyway, and we didn't allow the surroundings to dictate what the outcome would be. Only when we accepted them, that when they become a way of life. Being without is a temporary condition, but poverty is a state of mind. We were without many of times, but we knew it was just for the moment.

Sometimes you must take that chance. Don't try to figure out all the stops. If you wait for all the lights to turn green before you leave, you will never get out of the driveway. You must get in the car and start driving, and when the light is red, you stop until it turns green. You will eventually arrive at your destination. Capture the moment you know that presents the opportunity; yes the one at hand. We knew these times were forever around us, and the situation that was in place to dictate our destiny the law. In our particular case the law, known as the Jim Crow. One certainly had to learn how to live free, because the lawlessness of the land of the free sure didn't help us. For quite some time, even as we speak throughout this great land, I still can't see the real picture of freedom. But when you are born into a life of struggling, dealing with harsh treatments and racial injustice that causes tremendous tension, which prevent you from enjoying real freedom, you must know how to live free. Most of the tension was caused by the presence of the nightriders, which was the KKK.

Now here's a group that kind of stays in the shadows of this culture, and I can't find one good thing these people have ever done, anything for anyone at anytime. But they've been moving around through out society for quite some time, and yes they probably are here to stay. Basically they are a nocturnal group meaning of the night in the night.

"The Rise and Fall of Jim Crow"—PBS

A Brief Part of History, by Richard Wormser

Six Confederate veterans originally organized the Ku Klux Klan in the winter of 1865–66 in Pulaski, Tennessee, as a social club. In the beginning, the Klan was a secret fraternity club. Rather than a terrorist organization (Ku Klux was derived from the Greek "Kuklos," meaning "circle.") The costume adopted by its members (disguises were quite common) was a mask and white robe and high conical pointed hat. First organized in Tennessee, the Klan spread to every state in the South, which included mayors, judges, and sheriffs, as well as criminals. Now talking about the "leopard not losing its spots.

This is a prime example of that statement. One would think they all were criminals.

According to the founder of the Klan, it had no malicious intent in the beginning. Well, this is what truth means to some, so I thank him for letting us in on that part of the truth.

The Klan grew quickly and became a terrorist organization. Hello! "Like it wasn't at the beginning" It attracted former Civil

War generals such as Nathan Bedford, the famed cavalry commander whose soldiers murdered captured black troops at Fort Pillow. The Klan spread beyond Tennessee to every state in the south and included, again, mayors, judges, and sheriffs, as well as common criminals—pretty much like now. The Klan systematically murdered black political leaders. They beat, whipped, and murdered thousands, and intimidated tens of thousands of others from voting. Blacks often tried to fight back, but they were outnumbered and out gunned.

While the main targets of Klan wrath were the Political and social leaders of the black communities, blacks would be murdered for almost any reason. Men, women, and children, aged and crippled, were victims. A 103- year-old woman was whipped, as was a completely paralyzed man. In Georgia, Abraham Colby, an organizer and leader in the black community, was whipped for hours in front of his wife and children. His little daughter begged the klansman," Don't take my daddy away." She never recovered from the sight and died soon after. In Mississippi, Jack Dupree's throat was cut, and he was disemboweled in front of his wife, who had just given birth to twins. Klansmen burned churches and schools, lynching teachers and educated blacks. Black landowners were driven off their property and murdered if they refused to leave. Blacks were whipped for refusing to work for whites; for having intimate relations with white women; for arguing with whites; for having jobs whites wanted; for reading a newspaper; for having a book in their homes; or for simply just being black. Klan violence led one black man to write: "We have very dark days here. The colored people are in despair; the Rebels boast that the Negroes shall not have as much liberty now as they had under slavery. (And I ask, when did slavery end for blacks?) If things go on thus, our doom is sealed. God knows it is worse than slavery."

A few state governments fought back. In Tennessee and Arkansas, Republicans organized a police force that arrested Klansmen and carried out executions. In Texas, Governor Edmund Davis organized a state police unit. 40 percent of whose officers were black. The police made over 6,000 arrests and stopped the Klan. Armed groups of blacks and whites fought or threatened Klansman in the North and South Carolina. The federal government also exerted its influence, empowering federal authorities with the Enforcement Act of 1870 and 1871. Klan activity ended by 1872 and disappeared until it was revived again in 1915." Here is another question: why were they alloyed to continue when everybody knew what their purpose was?

It seems rather timely; when slavery was declared illegal in 1865, the Klan was beginning. I cannot find anything on record where these people have ever made any worthwhile contribution to society, but the very groups that are always in the crosshairs of their scope are forced to pay taxes for their protection when they are marching in protest for something. According to public account, the Klan is operating in all 50 states today, and nothing is ever said about it. I wonder how many of our elected officials now are holding membership cards? Because it seems to me that a person or a group of people, with the only purpose in mind is murdering, lynching and torching, should not have the right to continue these practices.

We were forced to live with physical and mental abuse, brutality, inhumane treatment, poor living conditions, just to name a few right here in this country. Where freedom was a part of that constitutional package we received. But soon you start to wonder, what happened and why. Well then you get hit with a big dose of reality that this wasn't going to get any better. This was just a regular day in the Peach State, and many other states throughout this free nation.

JIM CROW; WHAT IS IT?

It was a policy that was practice used for keeping segregation and the acts of discriminating against blacks in place without question. You know those six famous words—"we've always done it this way"—and it didn't even bother them the least. Now here again is my question. Why was Jim Crow allowed to continue when we were a free people? Now I am talking in the 1940s and beyond, and slavery was made an illegal act of the law in 1865. I just see something badly wrong with this picture. The people that were then and still are elected to protect all of our rights are these same people making sure the thing stayed just like they always were.

As the Massacre of Rosewood Florida in the early 1920s, this and many others such brutal attacks on a people just for having been born black, I would think those elected official just stood by and did nothing, and they are just as responsible as the ones who were doing the acts. This is why the very word "freedom" seems so unreal to me. So is what we see freedom, or is it just an illusion?

The first time I remember hearing an election campaign was around 1948. The candidate was Mr. Herman Eugene Talmadge. He was born on a farm near Mc Rae, Telfair County, Georgia, August 9, 1913. Talmadge attended the public school in Mc Rae. He received a law degree from the University of Georgia at Athens in 1936. He was admitted to the bar in 1936 and practiced law in Atlanta Ga. Talmadge volunteered for service in the United States Navy in 1941, saw extensive action in the pacific theater, and attained rank of lieutenant commander. He was discharged in November, 1945. Upon the death of his father, Governor-elect Talmadge was elected to the governorship by the state legislature in 1947. He served sixty-seven days, then vacated the office due to a decision of the state supreme court. He was elected in September 1948, to fill the unexpired term. Talmadge was re-elected in 1950 and served until January 1955; farmer; elected as a Democrat to the United States Senate. In 1956; re-elected in 1962, 1968, and 1974 and served from January 3,1957, to January 3, 1981. An unsuccessful candidate for re-election in 1980; denounced by the Senate in 1979 for financial misconduct. Chairman committee on Forestry and Agriculture (Ninety-second through Ninety-fifth Congresses), Committee on Agriculture, Nutrition, and Forestry (Ninety-fifth and Ninety-sixth Congresses); resumed the practice of law. Was a resident of Hampton, Ga., until his death on March 21,2002; buried on family farm near Hampton, GA. One thing is hard for me to understand is how he was representing the people of the state of Georgia, and he was a plantation owner with slaves at the very time he was elected. But another amazing thing about this outstanding public servant is how he arose through the ranks in the United States Navy to the rank of lieutenant commander in just four years of service?

Now please tell me, whom was he serving? These people then and now are elected to keep the scales of justice equally balanced for all citizens of this free land. (Seems like a miscarriage of justice to me.) We know he was a lawyer, and as for as I know, most of them are today.

Failure to attain the just, right, or desired result: a miscarriage of justice And / or contempt of court A feeling of disdain for anything considered mean, vile or worthless; the state of being despised; disgrace. Willful disobedience to or open disrespect for the rules or orders, of a court or legislative body; contempt of court. Because what they were doing was in direct violation of the law they all swore to uphold. They said, "Ignorance is not an excuse for the violations of the law," but what happens when you are not ignorant of the law and still violates it? Most of them then were, and now, are lawyers, and you ask why I say freedom is an optical illusion? To be subjected to a law that was made by a few people to rule over another unfairly, just because of skin color, or because of religious belief, or any other unjust reason. I thank we need to re think this freedom thing and see if there was something over looked, or we just missed, or is it just an illusion? But remember where we were. Do I see any change now? No, what I see is things just changed around. But the thing that bothers me is, who could those people be, that were elected to protect all citizens from such grievous treatments, and still allowing this to continue?

Dad and all of the other blacks were not so concerned about the present, because that was very well in place. Their concerns were more for the future. See, everybody's concern was everybody's concern—this is how we existed. But what kept us from becoming retaliatory? It wasn't because we were afraid; it was that we were taught that we must combat hate with love, and there's nothing in between. You either love or you hate, and if you choose not to love, then you become the other hater, so what have you achieved?

Life is a daily making of choices, and with each choice

comes a possible chance for error. The more choices you make, the greater the chance for error. But the greatest error of all is not making the choice. Then when the choice is finally made, be prepared to stand by that choice. So, what were our parents doing? They were teaching us a lesson for life and not for death, and I mean death as separation. Why am I mentioning this? Do I want anyone to think what we experienced living in Georgia was so bad? You're absolute right it was. But the point I want to make is how we were taught to handle it; that wasn't with hate but with love. If that was not the case, I don't want to think what the outcome would have been. That wasn't a lesson just for that moment; that was a lesson for life. Now remember, just because someone do you wrong, does not forfeit their right to be respected Alton Harvey Sr. (2004) Ralph Waldo Emerson; wrote; "If you put a chain around the neck of a slave, the other end fastens itself around your own."

What happened during those times was just stepping stones for where we are today. I'm a person with great optimism about the future of our country, only if all of us are willing to take a shot at trying to make a difference. By becoming involved with the affairs of our communities. Starting with the smallest part of any community, your next door neighbor and get involved in your block and become accountable to each other on a daily basis, by using the same principles we used—the principles of love. Trust me, it works. I read somewhere that "Evil is not a problem but a lesson that carries an opportunity." How I wish we would take a glance back once and awhile, just to see where we've come from and how we did it. Use something of the past, and start rebuilding a brighter feature, so we will give the feature generations a better chance at carry on.

"If you plant a grain, you will reap a bushel; if you plant a bushel, you will reap a field. But if you plant an idea, you will secure an entire generation." Alton Harvey, Sr., 2004

I am committed to giving not all I can, but whatever it takes to make things better; no, not for me or just someone who looks like me, but for the betterment of humanity.

After all, I feel I owe something just for living in such of a tremendous era in this nation's history. This way my testimony of how the love or God through his Son Jesus Christ, down thru generations of Christians, taught me how to love even when it wasn't in a loving situation, yes, there were other options.

But the foundation had already been laid, and our part was the easiest part of all.

All we had to do was just build on that foundation the foundation of our freedom is the Constitution, and the Declaration of Independence, and the amendments.

There weren't many choices for us, so Dad would take whatever was available and make the best of it.

We didn't have the choice of very many places to live. Daddy had to consider the land, and if it would be good for growing all the kind of crops we planted. It was believed the more we planted, the more we would be able to share. Well that wasn't the case. Of course we did not expect to have all of the amenities such as gas, lights, and two baths tubs. The bathing situation was the ole #3 galvanized tub and a wash pan; we took a bath every Friday night unless we were really dirty. If not then, it was just the wash pan, because water was a very special commodity. The toilet was an outhouse; for night use it was a ten-bucket. Some had lids to cover them. For the more extreme use, these were called "slop jars" to carry us thru the night. Oh yeah, they were the first things to take care of in the morning, because they would be making plenty of noise. There was no two-car garage and no electricity in our part of the hood. We just clarified the indoor plumbing. The entire black race living in the South—it didn't matter where—was really experiencing the true meaning of equality, and equal rights. All of us were treated equal under the law the Jim Crow. Every black person was considered equal but it was equally bad. The ones that weren't black had the right to treat all blacks equal, and the problem with this is, the same thing. What happened to freedom? You know, the freedom we were supposed to have gained in 1865. I truly can't see anything different now, except the signs are not posted anymore, but every thing else is still pretty much the same.

From Sun-Up till Sun-Down

My day would began at five o'clock a.m. and end when it was too dark to see. The alarm clock would sound each morning at about five a.m. (a rooster). You might say that's not so bad, but for a five-year-old child, that's bad. The first thing for me, getting a fire started in the winter and fall. The summer was just fine because it would be seventy or eighty degrees and sometimes more at seven in the morning. Then milking the cows, most of the time we had three cows, Fred would milk one and sometimes two, just to give me a hand, that's just like him always looking out for his brothers. Then he would go on to feed the mules and get them ready for whatever was going on, because there was always something for us to do. This is the life of a farmer. Most of our duties were pretty much repetitive. That's the way it was on the farm, and I'm sure it still is to some degree.

The landowners, who were nothing but slave masters, were responsible for providing all of the equipment and material needed for growing a crop. The farmer was to do all of the work, and it was enough of that to go around. This still wasn't a bad idea, until time for gathering or harvesting, and the selling part.

That's when the stuff really hit the fan. Here is where that sharing part got separated from the cropping. This was the way all of the landowners did it. We worked year after year, and it was always the same, maybe next year, but that year never arrived. What would happen when gathering time came; all of the crops were picked and brought to town where all of it would be weighed. The weigh master, would contact the plantation owner and let him know the crop had been gathered and weighed. Then the plantation owner would come to town without the farmer knowing of his coming, not that it would make any difference. After that visit had been made, he would come to the farmer's house whenever he chose with the results which would always be the same, in our case, well boy, talking to Daddy, you all did a good job, you broke even, maybe next year you might get a little something, but that year never arrived. But we kept chasing the American dream; you know, the one. Work hard and have what you want, and let the bells of freedom ring for all people.

In the off-season, late fall, and early winter, it seemed like Daddy would hardly ever be at home. He would go where he could work for money. There was never any problem for him finding work. The problem was getting to and from. But just hold on even in the south with God all things are possible. Because not so very long after that, Dad did get a 1938 Chevrolet almost like new, and oh my goodness, this was the "bee's knees." Everybody would rejoice for each other's prosperity. This wasn't just at the Harleys house but throughout the South. Daddy had a very good reputation for being a good hard worker. There were many landowners who needed workers to help them do their farming, and that's where the sharecroppers would make some money. There were quite a few men with very large farms and no one to work them. They would hire people to help, and this would give us a chance to go somewhere else and do the same things. But it was always good because we knew Daddy would be getting paid for our labor.

Now be reminded we were making minimum wages, which was just above nothing. This is where Dad would have monies when we all go to town and for buying different things, which wasn't too many things we needed to buy, because we grew our own food. "Ok, cry baby," what's all the fuss about not getting paid? We work all those years and never received any pay, and this was one of the things we supposed to have gained as a free people, to receive composition for our labor.

But we didn't know Daddy was saving train fair, so one day he would get his family away from that way of life.

Mom made most of our clothes, and a lot of things were sent to us from Daddy's sisters who lived in Chicago. Aunt Brownie would be the one to get everything sent off, and she would make sure everybody would have as much as the next one. Nobody would be left out, and this was a lot of fun for all of us. Sometimes Daddy would cry because it would always be at the times when we needed it the most. This was one of so many blessings this Harvey family enjoyed. Mom and Dad would start picking out things that other families could use. See, it was not if they needed something or if they would accept it, because all of us were in need for something. But the thing was, we all helped each other, this is how we survived through these very hard and difficult times. "But hard times make soft hearts, and soft hearts make strong and kind people." Alton Harvey, Sr., 2004.

The Heart of a Servant

(My Mother, Kira L. Harvey)

When it rained, which was quite frequent in the rainy season, and living in the backside of what seemed like God's country, because He was the only one who knew it was there, but it was home. After the rain, the red clay dirt roads were really bad for walking, and even the mules sometimes would break their legs. That would be bad in more ways than one. Walking became quit difficult. The wagons made tracks in the mud, and the few cars that traveled the roads made their tracks. When that muddy road dried, it was something like concrete. Then the convicts were the ones who kept the roads and ditches maintained. So many times when they were coming to work on the roads near our home, one of the officers would let the families know that they would be around for so many days. This was to say these men were somewhat dangerous. When they arrived, Mom would go to the guard and ask if she could cook dinner for them while they were there. I never knew a time when he didn't gladly welcome her offer. Most of the time there would be I believe eight or more men plus the guards, which was most of the time two. Every day at noon, we would take the food to the crew. Sometimes they would be working right in front of our house. When they were farther away, one of the guards would come with the truck and get the food and take it back to the men.

And the guards would tell Mom, "Lady all the gang and us (meaning the guards), show do thank you far watchie did for us" and this would go on until they finished and this would happen each time they were working around our house. She would put so much effort in making sure the food was ready when mid-day came so they had their dinner, and you could see how she enjoyed doing it for them. Now these were men in shackle and chains. They were chained together about six feet apart. They would sing what were known as chain gang songs. There were no words, just humming. All of them were dressed in the traditional white with black stripes, and they all were treated the same. In most cases, that wasn't good. I don't know how the non-black prisoners were treated because the white convicts weren't working alone beside the blacks. Even in crime, segregation was still present. This was the way Mom was through her life. It just looks if it was a lesson in every thing they did then; whether it was from our parents or some one else, the message was always the same.

With our parents, the joy was always in the giving. Dad said, Give today, and that giving must continue until everyone has enough. This is what he taught, and this is what he did. But we weren't always on the giving end when we needed something. There was always someone there to help us.

Now this illusion of being free came clear to me long before I realized what was happening, and grandmamma Ethel, and many others didn't ever experience anything but slavery.

Slavery was declared illegal in 1865, and slave labor was one of the things that was abolished—or was it? Our dictionary defines freedom this way as the state of being free or at liberty rather than in confinement, or under physical restraint, exemption from external control, the power to determine action without restraint. Political or national independences, personal liberty: slaves who bought their freedom. Exemption; immunity: freedom from fear. The absence of or release from ties or obligation. Ease or facility of movement or action, frankness of manner or speech a liberty taken, civil liberty as opposed to subjection, to an arbitrary or despotic government the right to enjoy all the privileges, or special rights, of membership in a community. The right to frequent enjoys or use at will. The reason I gave all these definitions is because it's important to me to know if these things I thought we were supposed to have gained in 1865 was true, or if I wanted something nobody else had.

Heritage of the Ancient Ones

(HTTP://WWW.SEMINOLETRIBE.COM/HISTORY/BRIEF.SHTML)

Momma Ethel was born April 13, 1885. This is the tribe she came from. As I remember, she stood about 5' 7, but to my short eyes, she stood at least 10' tall and weighed about 150. She was part Native American (the Seminole Tribe). This tribe is one of the very first people in the southeastern part of North America.

For thousands of years before the coming of Europeans to southeastern North America, perhaps as many as 400,000 of the ancestors of the Seminoles built towns, villages, and complex civilizations across the vast area. After 1510, when the Spaniards began to explore and settle in their territory, disease killed many of these people, but they were never destroyed or conquered as so many of the white men's history books proclaim. The survivors amalgamated across the peninsula of Florida and continued their lives. Sadly, the story of Florida's first native people and the 12,000 plus years that they cared for this land is largely untold. Even more frightening, they have begun to fade from our memories entirely. Due to Florida's geographic location in North America, these natives bore the brunt of the invading armies of

the Spanish, French, and English. In the 16th century, when the
first English speakers entered the area of the Southeast that is
now Florida. In 1763, they found many of these survivors from
tribes such as the Euchee, Yamasee, Timugua, Tequesta, Abala-
chi, and Coco. Hundreds of others, living as free people across
the head of the Florida peninsula, on the Alachua savannah the
area now known as Alachua country. In masko'ki, the core language, its Siminoli meant that they were free people, because
they had never been dominated by the Spaniards or the English
interlopers. In the Hitchiti dialect, of Maskoki, today known as
the Mikisuki, the separate tribal affiliation and just call them all
Semionlies, or Seminoles. Farther north, in the area now known
as Georgia, English traders who had begun to settle in 1690,
found many other Maskoki tribes along low-lying creeks. Especially the Oconi and Ogichi Tribes. Once again ignoring the
realities of the natives' lives, they began to refer to these people
all across the southeast just as "Creeks." With the end of the
American Revolutionary War and the creation of the untitled
states, in 1784, white settlers moved steadily southward into the
Spanish and former English colonies. It became more and more
obvious that a clash between white immigrants and the native
inhabitants of the land would take place sooner or later. This
began to be a concerted policy of taking or buying land from the
native tribes in the Northeast and Atlantic seaboard states. By
1813, some of the Maskoki tribes in Alabama rose up against the
white settlers and against those that supported white settlement.
This conflict, known as the Creek War of 1813–14, was disastrous
to the cultural relatives of the Seminoles.

Momma Ethel had high cheekbones. She looked as if she
had been hewn out of the side of a mountain. Her skin was very

dark. It seemed bronze with a very soft glow, and her hair was about to her lower shoulder, mixed grayish like silver and black; more gray than black. She always wore it platted in two large braids, one on each side of her head. Her cheekbones were highly pronounced. She also had squared shoulders; I thought she could balance the world about them. Her eyes were a soft brown with heavy gray eyebrows. Her eyes sat deep in the sockets of her skull. They seemed to shine with a light of pure love, and she spoke with soft words that would always bring comfort. She was a very kind person and full of wisdom. Her teeth were stained from snuff and tobacco. (Virginia Slims, "you've' come a long way, baby" had not yet come on the seen.) Her hands were large, and they showed signs of many years of very hard and harsh labor. I though she stood taller than life. Her right jaw was disfigured; that came from her being beaten because she refused the advances of her slave master. The vanes on her hands and arms were very large. They looked as if you could see the blood running through them. She didn't talk much about that part of her life. I think she didn't want to give us a negative impression about anyone, or just couldn't stand to revisit such a dark and bitter past. She always kept a big smile on her face that would just bring the light of joy to see her. Most of the time, she would hum this tune "Nobody nose de troubles I seen." I now believe some of the smiles were used as a disguise to cover up the pain of a very bitter past, but the memories of a brutal and rough life were always present.

She reminded me of those mother hens that would always protect their chicks, even with their own lives. I remember one day she and I had gone to meet the rolling store; we had to walk about three or four miles to the main road. It was very cloudy that morning with a pretty strong wind blowing, but that was quite common for that time of year. Returning from the store, a tornado came through. This was very common for the summer months, because we had no weather forecast. The skies were bright red from the dust where the winds had swirled it up, and it seemed like as the saying goes "out of nowhere" came this very strong wind. Sounding like many rushing waters, their were trees flying all around us. Momma took my hand, and we ran as fast as we could. We got to a ditch, she threw me down to the ground face down and she fell down over me, with our heads upward on the side of the ditch so the water would not over flow us. I remember her saying, "Lord, keep my boy safe and let nothing happen to him." I cannot remember hearing her say, "Lord, take care of me." This seemed like it took forever, but not so long after the storm passed over, we completed our journey home without a scratch.

THIS IS PUBLIC INFORMATION

The United States Congress appointed a commission to study reparation a proposal for Blacks and/or African Americans. Introduced in house HR 40 The 108th Congress January 7, 2003, they found that there were approximately 4,000,000 Blacks and/or African Americans, and their descendants, was enslaved in the United States and the colonies that became the United States. From 1619 to1865; the institution of slavery was constitutionally and statutorily sanctioned by the government of the United States from 1789 through 1865; the slavery that flourished in the United States. That constituted an immoral and inhumane deprivation of blacks and/or African Americans' life, liberty, citizenship rights. Cultural, heritage and language, and denied us the fruits of our labor. My question still remains:

what took this investigation as long as it did because the problem is not at all new. Once again the elected officials that were elected to oversee these laws, and to make sure every citizen was protected and given all rights under the law—what are they doing? Or maybe the Jim Crow law is the way they want it to be. The treatment of black American slaves in the colonies and the United States including the deprivation of their freedom, exploitation of their labor, and destruction of their culture, language, religion families, and there very way of life. So Mamma Ethel and many others free Americans that was given their freedom under the United States constitution, for them freedom really was an optical illusion.

Mamma Ethel was a very strong-built woman. Especially her hands and arms, and I understand why. She worked hard plowing fields, cutting down trees to make more fields, toting water to wash clothes and water for all the livestock. We must remember this was not for her; this was for O Massa is what they said. Massa. After she finished, she would have to walk many miles home at night, sometimes in the rain and cold and through the woods to get home, just to find things to do for her two children. That would be Mom and her brother (Uncle Charlie). Mom told us one time Mamma said to her, "Kira if anything happens to me, you have to take care of buddy Mom's brother, because I don't think I'll make it through the night. She was totally drug-out tired. Now this is pure speculation. Possibly that day she could have been made to pull a small plow, and the reason this is been mentioned because there were places around there were slave masters would have those human beans doing the things the mules did.

Mom said she had never seen Mamma that tired before.

What a way to live, in a free nation, the land of the free, day after day. Cutting wood with an ax was just another part of life on the farm We cut wood for cooking, wood for heating the house, wood for heating water to wash clothes and for bathing, and where did this wood come from? Of course we had to go into the woods and cut down trees and saw them into pieces to fit the fireplace and the stove, which naturally were different sizes. Chopping cotton, peanuts, and all that other stuff. It seems like there was always some chopping going on. Planting the garden, which was a very big job within itself. Daddy thought his responsibility was to grow enough food for everybody, and I think we did, and in doing so, it taught us a great deal in the approach to living a free life. By not becoming selfish and we still thrive on these principles today. Hard work gave us more than just our hands filled with corns, calluses, busted knuckles, cut feet from rocks, glass and thorns. Somehow at the end of the day, none of those things was important. What did it do for us; it made us realize the needs of others are more important than our own. It also taught us how to recognize that need and try to fix it, and not think about the reason, just see that the need was taken care of. Daddy told us he didn't want to hear, we'd done our best. He said you must do whatever it takes to get the job done, because just doing your best might not be enough. As I venture back some years later, I realize he always had the well being of others in mind, and I think some of his attributes are in all of us today. I think we need to clarify something here; I don't want to leave anyone thinking, "Man, does he think this family of his is the cream of the crop?" Quite the contrary, this family just knows how to love and care, that doesn't mean just each other, or when it's most convenient for our schedule. It also means when its hurts, and to love those who might try to harm you in some way. We know how to call for help, but most of all, we are always ready to answer the call when someone is calling for our help. When we go, we go together. Yes, we're like most; we're just little tadpoles trying to become frogs. Together just like frog eggs

Those that lived it firsthand could only experience living in the swamps of a very uninhabited part of anywhere. One idea that came to me as I started writing, and how we as a family continue the togetherness of our past learning's, was the frog's egg.

When the frogs lay their eggs, they lay them just a few inches below the water surface attached to a log, or to the side of the bank, with some sunlight. The eggs are just little black spots, look something like grains of black pepper in cased in a jell-like embryo. As long as that embryo remain intact, at due time the eggs will hatch into tadpoles, and then some will eventually become frogs, and that is what they suppose to be. Somehow we were able to keep that embryo, which in our case was love, from being torn apart. None of us was taken by all of the negative things that awaited each and every one of us. This is why we remembered how everybody looked out for everybody. We have kept that concept all of our lives.

When we go to do something, we don't leave until the job is finished.

Brother Fred and I are the only ones left that have any memories of our life on the farm. All of the others who would have had memories to share are already with the Lord, and that's the best part about that. We will talk more about them further on up the road.

I do want to mention that some of the other landowners treated all of us very well. On one occasion, Dad, Fred and I were doing some work for this person his name was Mr. Pete Crawford. He asked Dad, Douglas if things were reversed, how would you treat me? Daddy said, "Well, Mr. Crawford, I would not want you to go through what we have to go through, but if they were, I would treat you like a man." Mr. Crawford just lowered his head and walked away. That just sent a charge of joy right through me, and that was something I have never forgotten. Because I just knew Daddy had won that round. Just because your situation isn't so good, or as good as you might think it should be, doesn't mean everybody's should be as bad.

Somehow this might sound like one of those other country that's in the news where freedom was not a part of their life. Well, neither was it a part of ours, but the difference is we are living in a free country; or is this "freedom just an illusion"?

Any and every kind of hard work you can think of, I've done my share and somebody else's, too. I know this seems like story-telling; well, it is. But this story happens to be true. I've' learned over the years that freedom isn't just a beautiful word; it's a word that helps make life more beautiful, when freedom is there. But if you never had the chance to enjoy being free, you can't compare it to living free. If you have learned how to live free, then you don't miss not being free. But if you never learned how to live free, then being free has no real value.

You know how we have been told for so long that we are free? Well, I am sorry to say we've been given a picture that has convinced us that the image we see is real. The difference is, we as a society never had anything to compare it to; this is why to me it seems like an illusion. That's what bothers me the most. Our lives on the farm in Georgia, living as slaves, but all the while we were told that we were free. I believe that is called an oxymoron. Here comes the knuckle ball. Once again, the people who were elected to stand guard over the laws of our land and make sure all citizens would enjoy the rights given under the laws of the United States Constitution and the amendments; these were the same people that were doing these horrible things to us then and still are today. This is why I don't see this picture getting any clearer.

It's hard to believe that some of the congressmen and senators then had plantations, and it wouldn't be a surprise to me if it would be known that there are still some today. They are still representing a free people, and I ask, which people?

I was born April 13, 1939. The day I got here, Mamma was 54 years old, so I thought I had somewhat of a edge over the rest of the group when I realized Mama had the charge of special operations. She would oversee the health and welfare of the Douglas and kira Harvey family.

Now there were already five of us. My brother Edward, he was born May 8, 1942. I don't remember him until later on, but when I learned I had to take care of my little brother, I felt like his big brother and this relationship lasted for always. Now I had a big brother and I was a big brother, and that was all good. Ed and I grew closer as we grew older. I taught him how to shoot marbles. This was the most popular game for the smaller boys, and the older boys played marbles to.

October 7, 1945, there was another announcement: "It's a girl." Sally Doris arrived, and nothing changed. It was just another day on the farm. Seems like somewhere between all of the farming at home and the shooting and booming in Europe, Mom and Dad were real busy having babies. This was number seven, but when one of us got sick with colds, cuts, scrapes, sometimes broken bones, mumps, poison ivy, poison oak, boils, measles, chicken pox, and who knows how many other things could of happen. Mamma Ethel would just go into the woods, which was just beyond the yard, and get some roots from various kind of trees and boil them into a tea and give it to us and soon after we were good to go, and she never mist diagnose a case. So go ahead and ask how she could do this without any background knowledge in medicine. And my answer is, "I don't know," but I do know it worked. Now this was not one of those cure-all concoctions, but it was a treatment for whatever the problem was. She just seemed to know what tree to consult for the solution. It was not very often that people had to visit a doctor. There were only two doctors in Cuthbert, but most of the time one of the doctors would just make a visit once or twice a year to see how everyone was doing without charge. I think just that close-community-type lifestyle and the love we had for each other, although our neighbors sometimes were miles apart, but the concern for each other and momma Ethel's herbs, kept everyone around her as healthy as she could. But there wasn't as much sickness as there is now. I wonder what happened. Sometimes she (Momma Ethel) would just leave without any of us children knowing anything about her whereabouts. There would be times she would be gone for two or three weeks. We learned much later she would go back to her "master," whoever he was and worked, because it was said she had ran away, but why would a free woman, living in a free country would still owe a slavery debt? What part of this United States Constitution applies to these people? Please remember, slavery was declared illegal under the constitution twenty years before she was even born. How could this be? Well, this illusion gets even clearer when one of our former presidents, Jimmy Carter, was serving in the oval office, it was "reported there was black citizens living on a plantation he owned living as slaves, and he denied knowing about it although it was his property." These are some of the things that make me wonder whether what I see is real or is in fact an illusion. But if one checks the civil rights records of all of this nation's presidents, you will find just a few that supported any bill that was centered on or around the rights of black Americans. But again, former president William Jefferson Clinton did give a public apology for the treatments of black Americans. But when ask about a proposal for reparations for African Americans, he was not in favor of such a thing. That was the end to his contribution to this matter. I wonder if there was ever a time when he served as governor of the state of Arkansas when he had the chance to execute the law fairly for the benefit of all people; if so, how did he do it? Just a thought.

"The evidence of a processed thought is found in a done deed." Alton Harvey Sr.

It's just kind of strange that every other so-called minority group gets some kind of recognition who has been mistreated except the blacks in this land called America. Or what we call freedom was not meant for us, and this thing is so deeply engraved into the fabric of our well justly, and totally equal, none discriminatory society. I hear quite often that there isn't anything wrong, and these are well-mannered, law-abiding American citizens. The American lifestyles of my Caucasian counterparts right now do not see there is a problem. And some may ask why. Well, I think it's because the picture we are given looks like freedom, but it's just an illusion. When one is given one side, and one is given another side, but either side is not equal, that's when the illusion becomes so clear. Now I am an American. If I were asked if I see change, I would say no. What I see, it's just changed around. "If you take a container of water, you have just water. If you freeze that water, you have made the same thing look different, but it's still water." This is why I say this freedom is an illusion, but this illusion gets greater; just wait. US senator of the state of New York Hillary Rodham Clinton—yes, the same one who once lived at the White House—was asked at a town hall meeting if she was in favor of reparations. She answered with a ready reply, "No." She added, "This was a part of our history that should be forgotten, and it's time we should move on and focus on the future." I think without a clean past—and there is quite a lot need cleaning— it's not possible to build a bright future. But she then said, and I quote but the terrible thing and I agree with her on this, "The atrocious crimes that the Jewish people suffered in Europe are something we should never forget." And it's still a present topic today. But what strike me so strange is that this country had no part in those crimes and the horrific torturing of all those people. But the ones against the black citizens, who they did and still are doing, we should just push them to the side because Mrs. Clinton, one of our honored senators, said she sees no need to discuss past matters. So we should just close the books of history and seal the pages of a forgotten and bitter past, no matter how atrocious and inhumane and the brutality it was, and still is today. That seems like she still supports the Jim Crow system. It makes one wonder how some things although seems to be so related in some ways, lose all meaning in other ways. I guest it just depends on who is in the arena when the time comes to feed the lions.

I wonder why it's never mentioned how so many other people have migrated here from other parts of this world, but we, the African Americans, are the only ones who did not have a choice in coming here. We have been here for quite some time now, and we are still not welcome and accepted as American citizens. Reading Mrs. Clinton's Living History, which is a very good book, on pages 22 and 23 and I quote, "We visited black and Hispanic churches in Chicago's inner city for exchanges with their youth groups. In the discussions we had sitting around church basement, I learned that, despite of the obvious difference in our environments, these kids were more like me than I ever could have imagined. They also knew more about what was happening in the civil rights movement in the South. I had only vaguely heard of Rosa Parks and Dr. Martin Luther King, but these discussions sparked my interest. So, when Don announced one week that he would take us to hear Dr. King speak at Orchestra Hall, I was excited. My parents gave me permission, but some of my friends' parents refused to let them go hear such a 'rabble-rouser.' Dr. King's speech was entitled, 'Remaining Awake Through a Revolution.' Until then, I had been dimly aware of the social revolution occurring in our country, but Dr. King's words illuminated the struggle taking place and challenged our indifference: We now stand on the border of the Promised Land of integration. The old order is passing away, and a new one is coming in. We should accept this order and learn to live together as brothers in a world society, or we will all perish together." Seems like her thoughts might have changed. PBS—"From Swastika to Jim Crow: The Story" (http://www.pbs.org/itvs/fromswastikatojimcrow/story.html)

BLACK-JEWISH RELATIONS

Two People with very different backgrounds find love out of horror.

"Only months after Hitler seized power in 1933, Jewish intellectuals who had held prestigious positions in Germany's renowned universities were targeted for expulsion. Those who dared to oppose the edicts were met with brutal suppression. Often leaving with little more than the clothes on their back, many of these scholars fled to America, hoping to continue their academic careers. They soon found themselves in a strange and mysterious country, a nation reeling from the depression and ripe with anti-Gemitic and anti-German sentiment. While the most famous refugees, like Albert Einstein, were welcomed into the hallowed halls of Eastern academia, most of these refugee scholars faced an academic world that was aloof, if not down-right hostile. Much to their surprise, many of them were welcomed into a group of colleges that the vast majority of white American professors ignored—the historically all-black colleges in the South. For the black colleges including Howard University, Hampton Institute, and Tougaloo and Talladega colleges, the refugee professors provided the opportunity to add great talent to their faculty; for the professors, the arrangement provided a new home, a classroom of students eager to learn, and an insider's look at an America that few ever see. While most of these pairings between Jewish refugees and black colleges began as marriages of convenience, very often they blossomed into love matches for a lifetime. "They found a place where they could make a contribution, and they found a place where they could pursue their intellectual life, they found a place where they could make a difference."

Dr. Ismar Schorsch, chancellor, Jewish Theological Seminary, through interviews with several surviving academics and many of their former students, a fascinating story unfolds of men and women who found a true home in a community that, on the surface, was as remote as possible from the world they had known. Living in the rural South during segregation, the refugees didn't fit on either side of the line. Ostracized, from by their white neighbors, they socialized mostly within the university. If they invited their black students and colleagues home, they risked a visit by the Ku Klux Klan. "Dr. Manasse said when he first came to America as a freshly-minted Ph.D. from one of the most respected and revered institutions in Germany, perhaps in all of Europe, that he found it strange that he encountered nearly as much anti-Semitism here as he did in Europe. (Eugene Eaves, provost former student, North Carolina Central University) But professors and students shared a profound connection a common history of oppression and the knowledge of what it is like to be despised and persecuted on race or religion. Art professor Viktor Lawenfeld was interested in our inner feeling. We live a restricted life of segregation and discrimination, so art became the way that we could speak. Viktor chose Hampton because it was a black school. He understood racial prejudice in America and felt that he should cast his lot with those people who were working against racism." John Biggers, artist (former student, Hampton Institute.)

From the 1930s to the rise of civil rights and Black Power movements. ("From Swastika to Jim Crow" is a mesmerizing chronicle of Jim Crow America and a profoundly moving tale of two seemingly different groups- the formal, heavily accented European scholars and their young Black students who enriched each other's lives in ways still being felt today. http://www.pbs.orge/itvs/fromswastakatojimcrow/story.html.) Summer was always a fun time for us. We would go fishing and play baseball. Our activities were very minimal, and most of the things we did were just made up, but we found great entertainment in doing so. There wasn't much time for playing, anyway, but we learned to enjoy each other even while we worked. Oh, how we missed television then! "Yeah, right." What we had was just books and a radio, and to make a comparison with what's going on now, it's a whole world apart. Then it was having the ability to see things with your mind, and the impression of everything seems to have a more lasting value.

The sounds of war flooded the airways with the reporting of the warfare. Daddy and Mom and many others who had radios kept their ears close to the sound box that gave an update of the war. It was about three or four weeks later when the news got to the states—nothing like now. There would be a day-to-day replay of what has taken place and the casualties on either side. The advances and what hill or position had been taken, and guess what they did: when a town or any major defeat was made, well they mounted the American flag. Yes, the same one our congress and the supreme justices said it's ok to burn. I am still wondering just what part of this country they are representing. One of Daddy's brothers, the next to the youngest, was in that war. It was a great concern for the family about his safety. I remember Daddy would not go very far away to work. He wanted to stay as close to the radio as possible to hear the next update.

These were times when food was being rationed so the military could have enough. The good thing about this was we grew all the food we needed and then some, so we had plenty to give to others. It was said that the farmers were getting paid to help supply food for our troops, but we never knew anything about that. We were glad to take part in supporting our country. There were tokens issued to make sure nobody was getting more than the portions that were allotted for each family. A token was a penny-like object. I think it was made of some kind of wood. It was a dark reddish color. Daddy would give his to other people that didn't have a farm so everybody would have enough to eat. It seemed like we grew enough to feed most of the population, and the more we gave away, the more we had to give. It seemed like people were coming from far and near, and some would come very late, but that was ok. Daddy said some would come when they thought nobody would see them. More importantly, he said when you are serving, if it was always at a convenient time, something was wrong with your service.

Scrap metal of all kinds was very much in demand for making bombs and all other forms of weaponry. Everybody was in the business of recycling. It was a real need, and we all tried to supply that need. It was an ole geezer; we never knew his real name. Everybody called him Mr. Wash. He would have me help him make his scrap runs. We also called him the iron man. He drank all of the time. He had me drive him around after he was to drunk to drive. It's a blessing he didn't wreck and hurt himself. He was a complete misfit. The whites didn't want him around them, and he refused to live around us. He remained a very lonely man. Now this poor soul surely wasn't free. The automobile industry stopped making cars for three or four years, but that was not a big blow to most of us. But to see everybody involved in doing something for a real good cause was something within itself.

Moonshine stills were all over the place. Was it legal? Well, of course not, but these were ways most poor people had to survive. There were many pairs of shoes and clothes and food bought with that stuff; and besides, most of the costumers were those good old boys who did whatever they wanted to do.

WWII was almost over, and people were having parties, singing, dancing, and praising with great joy. Our uncle was still missing in action. I think now Daddy must have felt something, because he didn't have too much to say about his coming home. Military airplanes were forever around the place. One morning there was a plane flying very low, and it kept circling all around for maybe two or three hours. From our house to the town it was about ten miles, and this plane was flying so low we thought it was going to crash. But after a long time, it was announced on the radio that the plane had dropped a five-hundred- pound bomb near the lumber mill in town. It was too heavy, and the plane couldn't reach the right altitude. But they said it didn't pose any danger; that's why they were flying so low. It became a major event there.

The time for me to start my education had finally arrived. The school and church shared the same grounds. But to me, this was a very special time. I got the chance to walk to school, which was about seven miles from our house. I'd walked that same road many times before, but now somehow it seemed quite different. It seemed like we always lived farther away from everything than all of our friends, and walking was just what we did. When we went to town or church, the wagon would be our transportation until we finally got our first car. My classes consisted of the usual: reading, printing, spelling, math, geography, and science. Our school was one large room. Four grades wee taught simultaneously with no interruptions. There were only two teachers. My first teacher's name was Mrs. P. Johnson. She was a very caring, genuine person with the future of our lives in mind. The head teacher's name was Mrs. W. Taylor. Now this person was the "bee's-knees," and she didn't allow anyone to be denied a good education. This lady would go anyplace she thought she could find the most modern materials, and she would use her own money. See, the state was supposed to furnish the supplies, and they did, but they were all quite old and very raggedy. Pages were torn out, and there were markings from much earlier use. I never had a new book until much later. This building was old with a wood-burning stove for heat. It wasn't uncommon to have a snake join in. The kitchen connected to the stage. You could see the anger on the faces of Mrs. Taylor and Mrs. Johnson because they were trying to do a job without the proper materials, but they kept doing the same thing over and over. I think either one of the two would have driven all the way from town each day for just one of us. Cousin Otis would help them by taking all of the assignments papers over the weekend and grading them and send them back on Monday. The boys' responsibilities were to keep the school clean and keep wood for heating and cooking. We had to supply the school with food, which was cooked right in the school kitchen. On Monday the cook would have the next week's menu ready, and each person would take it home. On Friday we were to bring whatever was donated. The farmers would give the very most because we grew the food and we had more to give. It was never a question whether anyone didn't have anything to give or not, because there was enough to go around many times over. This gave all an equal part in the giving. So this is the way it was before I started school, and it was still going on when we left. I sometimes revisit those times, and I must admit those were some of the best times of my life, because what I learned then is exactly what I am sixty years later. Oh, something I must mention. Our classes were from 9:00 a.m. till 3:30 pm. But we were expected to be in our seats at 8:45. We started with the Lords prayer and then we would recite the Pledge of Allegiance. Oh yes, and the "board of Ed" (straps) would be applied to the backside of the body; that was a part of the regular curriculum. It wasn't a crime for the parents and teachers to teach the children to respect the authorities and property of others. So the "board of ed" was applied without objections. Back then, God was needed in our nation. But now in the minds of some, our society doesn't need God anymore or anywhere. Everybody can see what happened when prayer was taken out of the schools. It opened the doors for everything else to go in. Back then it was all about the involvement of everybody. From the first grade through the fourth, we walked to school; and from the fifth grade through the twelfth, we rode the school bus into Cuthbert. But we still had need for new books, which we never got. I never had a new school book, or one with all of the pages until 1951–2, when we moved to Michigan.

There were so many families I would like to talk about, but this would take another book just to give due acknowledgements to them. But this one must get due notice—the Jenkins family, three boys and two girls. The father's name Allie Sr.; the mother's name was Otis, and the children's names were Marilyn, Allie Jr., Elvin Neal, Annie, and Rushiel. Now this family probably touched more lives in that part of town than any other. There wasn't much money within the black families, but it never mattered. They were well educated, and they would try to help where help was needed. We are blood related to this family, and I am proud to have this close connection with them. The two parents and two sons are both home with the Lord, and the other three all are still hanging on. They are still the same, as I knew them years ago. Marilyn, Allie Jr., Annie, and Rush all became educators. Elvin, after a hitch in Korea in the United States Army, lived in Chicago for a few years. Then he returned back to his hometown in Georgia, and he became a paramedic. He also worked in one of the banks there. But shortly after, he was elected to the office of county coroners. Now the top three of them are retired, but I would guess that all of them are still involved in some kind of service to humanity. They all are very active in their local church. So it just seems like Daddy and Cousin Allie and many others were growing something other than cotton, corn, and peanuts. When the county started bussing black students, Cousin Allie got the job, and they could not have found a better person for the job of driving the bus. I don't think he even applied for the job he was chosen, and that was a win for everybody.

But our occasional counterparts had all of the new books and everything else they needed to obtain a good education like it was suppose to have been. But this is part of that freedom packet we received. So the only thing they had to do was learn, and that gap hasn't narrowed very much—"watcher think?"

But when it was time for farming, the boys didn't go to school because we had to work the farms. This was never addressed because the system was set up that way, and that's the way it was. But Cousin Otis would help anyone that wanted to learn. She would teach the boys in the evenings and on Saturdays if the parents would send their children to her. She did not want any pay; she just wanted all of us to learn. Now I hope you can see the premises of this freedom that we "all have," or maybe it is an illusion after all. Now our parents were no scholars, but they did their best in preparing us for the long haul. You probably are going to say, didn't your daddy say he did not want to hear about doing your best; how your best might not be good enough? He most certainly did. My dad went to the third grade, and my mother finished the seventh. With what they had to work with, I am very proud of the outcome of all nine children.

Well it was time again. February 19, 1947, Mom gave birth to another girl, Helen. This was really a joy. Now there are eight of us. Whenever there was an addition to our family, nothing changed. Everybody would just fill in and do what had to be done without being told. Dad always said to prepare for war in the time of peace. I'm much older now, and his teaching has had time to germinate. I have had the opportunity to test the wisdom he pasted on to me, and I can speak to the validity of that teaching. Life is full of all kinds of parts and pieces, and there's value in every thing. As we live day after day, we gather more and more pieces. After the accumulation and preparation, then comes the application. But if we don't understand what we have, just having it is meaningless. Until we realize what we've got, nothing will change. I realized quite a few years ago that we did have the ability to live a free life, whether we were given freedom or not. But if you chose not to live free, no proclamation can make you free.

I heard a story a long time ago. There was a lady, let's call her Anna (with no one in mind). After she had been freed from slavery, she desired to stay with her master, who was a very wealthy man. She had been given the small little maid's quarters, and after some time, her master became very ill and died. She was left to take care of the misses. Shortly after, the misses came to her door and said "Anna, you take this envelope and put it in a safe place." Anna said, "Yes, misses," and she hung it on a nail behind the front door. Shortly after misses passed away and Anna was left alone, Anna had spent all of her money and she was in great need. A small insurance policy had been purchased for Anna, and the insurance agent came to see if she wanted to surrender the cash benefits when he finished with the business at hand. As he started to leave, he noticed this envelope hanging on the nail. The appearance showed it had been there for quite some time. It had the appearance of something important, and he inquired about the contents. "Well," Anna said, "My misses gave that to me just before she died." He looked inside and discovered what Anna had was her master's entire estate in the form of an official will. Suddenly Anna became the richest person there. But until she realized what she had, Anna lived the life of a poor old woman.

One Saturday evening another family, which were also our cousins, the Shorter's, the father's name Randall, mother's name Maggie, and the children's names: Morris, Pauline, Theodore, Fluorine, Randall Jr., Essie, Willie, Elizabeth, Nathaniel and Booker T. One evening their house caught fire and burned down. There was no fire department, and the house was made of wood, so it was very dry. Within a very short time, it was just a pile of ashes. The only thing they had was what they were wearing. I thank God they had not gone to bed yet, because if they had, this story would have a very different ending. Now this family was one up on us in size. There were ten children, but only seven lived at home at this time, so that made things much better. The Harvey household became a total of twenty people. But absolutely nothing changed. After all the assessments had been made, Daddy said to cousin Randall, "There is nothing else for us to do now, so let's go home." Dousin Maggie asked how all could fit in one house. Daddy said the same way one family fit, just a little closer. But you know, God always has everything in place. See, all of us were already about the same size and same age. The first thing was to divide our clothes amongst everybody and get everybody ready to do whatever it took for us to live in the situation. Everything went just as always. By the next week, everybody knew what had happened, and then the celebration began. People all over got on the telephone and called everybody, "Yea right. What phone?" "Just kidding." But it wasn't but a very few days, and people from everywhere came with clothes for everybody, and I must mention this. There were plenty of white people doing as much as anyone else. They were very much involved with everything to help as was the blacks from start to finish, but ye see what was happening there, was not the whites being so bad as much as that system we was in. Because if the white families would show too much concern and compassion for blacks, then they would be visited by that group known as the KKK and be labeled as "nigger lovers." That was the worst plague they could have. It was already plenty of food because the

Lord had blessed us with a very healthy year before. There was a lot of pork meat, veggies, and corn for meal. Mom had plenty of preserves, chickens, and eggs, milk and butter, so everything was real good. That's what being blessed is for; just keep passing it on. All we had was not at all just for us. From the beginning, this lasted only about four or five months. One day there were some men cleaning the Debra away, and shortly after new lumber started to appear. Then a black carpenter came and made the form for the foundation. Next came a white man who was also a house builder. He started the frame work, then families from all around came to do whatever they could to help. It took about a month because people would do most of the work after our daily work was finished. Just like always, when you suffer some kind of misfortune, when it is restored it's better than before. It seem like as fast as it burned down, it was built back again. But this time they had a much larger house than the other one. And what did it cost the Shorter family? Absolutely nothing. This is the way we lived. We shared each other's pain, and we celebrated each other's good fortunes. Love kept us doing for each other and never got tired.

For our white counterparts which were indeed constitutionally free, but not at all able to live free, now once again if this freedom we see isn't an illusion, then why are so many of us struggling with just living free?

Fred and I had gone to practice baseball, which was about five miles from our home. Somehow it seemed like we always lived farther than everybody else. Walking was the second only way to get from place to place, but there was never was any thought about it. Shortly after we arrived at the ball diamond, we saw someone coming. I truly can't remember who this person was, but when we saw this person, we just knew what had happened. All he said was, "Boys, you need to go home right now." We ran most of the way back home and then realized just what had happened. Mama Ethel had passed. Mom was outside near the front doorstep with a very numb look on her face. Shortly after Daddy arrived as knowing what to find, this was I guessed the saddest day of our lives. By the time Daddy got home, all of us were crying. Mom had gone on the other side of the house. I'm sure she went there to have a moment of quiet prayer, because that's what they did in these and all other times. But I never saw her cry. I think maybe she needed to show us how people and families handle adversities. Then Dad got all of us together, and he just prayed. We held each other with the firmness that you could just sense everything would be all right. I think that's when we really learned just how this prayer business worked, learning at such early age how we must deal with different crises. We did learn how to cope with not having Mama around, but only in the physical. She is certainly with us in spirit. That tradition is the way this family deals with everything now. This was something different, seeing none of us children had ever experienced this before. I guess here is where I really started to understand the real importance of family unity and the strength gained from it. It's something like those frog eggs. Daddy started to affirm more so then than before, he said no matter what we become or where we go, "always" keep this family together, and that we have done and nothing has ever destroyed us, just like those frog eggs.

A Place I Remember

A True Story

They dangled from the top of those tall white oak trees like long braids of mangled gray hair, flowing from a very tall and slender lady. They were so long as if they were stretching their locks from the high heavens, with the ends finding a place to rest in the cold and murky waters below, with old fallen logs of driftwood that made a grim and slippery walk. Oh, how majestic was this place, with thick green and dried leaves; green vines like foliage covering the floor of the earth; some even with poison ivy.

These marshlands are found in much of the swampy parts of Georgia. What beauty can be found in such wet, cold, and mossy place, yet quiet, warm, and serene? It was a place where I could go and be alone with my dog. I think every boy had a dog then. His name was "Brown Foot," black with all four feet brown and when I was there, I could feel the comfort of the hollow swamp. Small bodies of water, standing as if it had no place to go as if it was an outcast from the main streams, you could always find these small bodies of water, some only four or five feet wide. A large person could easily jump across them at any given point. This place was full of life; it had many different kinds of fish and other water creatures, small and some not so small. There were jackfish standing motionless just a few inches from the top off the water. Dad said the crawfish and the puppy dogs helped keep the streams clean.

This place seemed almost like a garden of its own. There were raccoons sunbathing on a leafless limb at the highest point of the tree, and squirrels' nests in almost every tree. You could always hear the sound of a yellowhammer or redheaded wood-pecker drilling holes in a dried tree, with the bark scaled down to the ground. Oops, there's a huge water moccasin sliding into the water; the sound of bullfrogs croaking in one of the nearby ponds. There were large silk webs spun by spiders to trap their prey. A blue jay screaming, sounding like he's saying "scarce scarce" and another sounds as he's saying "take a little." There are many kinds of lizards crawling around these places, some jumping from one tree limb to another, there is one about twelve inches in length, bright green in color, with bright red skin under their necks. The sweet smell of honeysuckle would take away anything that might be frightful. I was always amazed to see how such contrast and yet so much beauty could bring such balance, like a high-wire artist finding the right balance to complete his stunt. I would visit this place simply because it always seemed so lonely and private, but it always welcomed anyone who wanted to visit. I felt like I was a visitor, yet I always found comfort. At the time I had never heard anything about a vacation, but now I think it was my imaginary vacation. There was a little hill just at the edge of the swamp. You could lie on your back, look through the trees, and find different shapes and images in the thick moss and tangled wild grape vines about the size of a man's upper arm. It was a place where I could just forget about whatever was going on around us; I guess I did wonder if everyplace was the same or if it was just where we lived. I hope everyone has a place like this old mossy swamp. I sometimes take a trip back in my memory and rejoin that very special moment of past but pleasant times. I hope you can visit this place with me or have a place of your own. Maybe we can visit each other's place sometime.

Now the ending of winter, the sounds of spring with the beating of iron plowing tools, is sharpening them for the beginning of another year of unending disappointments at the end of the year. Dad was about forty years old, and his physical condition was pretty good and always full of fun. He was a fairly small man in stature, about 5'5, and weighed about 140 lbs. His hair was short with a receding cowlick, but if an oxymoron is appropriate here, he was a little giant of a man. Mom, from a wife's point of view, Daddy diffidently was her guy. There was never any doubt about their love for each other, and they thought their children were gifts from God. But somehow things like size, shapes, and color never had that much of a meaning to us. We only saw Dad and Mom and just that. That was plenty enough for us. Dad would have the tools ready to get started when spring arrived. He would always plow the first row, as if he was reminding Fred and I nothing has changed from the last time, this is the way I want it to be done always. When that plow gouged down into the soil, it seemed like he was plowing up new life. The smell of fresh dirt just made it seem all worthwhile. Yesterday's troubles seemed so far in our memory as it had never happened.

The first row was to let us know how he expected the entire field to look. You might have thought he was plowing a plum line, as if we were going to lay a foundation for a building. As he would plow that first row, I would walk behind him, trying to step in his foot prints. But his steps were to long for my short legs. I stretched as far as I could, but I never was able to make it. Now I'm his senior in years when he passed on, but I'm sure I'm still not able to measure up to the steps of that "Small Giant" of a human being. I didn't realize the steps I was following then would be the paths I would someday walk. Oh, I only hope the path I leave for someone else to follow will be as straight as the one that led me to my place today. I often take a glance back just to see if I can see any crooks in that path I'm leaving. If someone were following me, would he have a path left for him as straight as mine was? He told us, "Don't pay too much attention on what people tell you. Just watch them, and they will reveal the truth in their walk. But you must remember they are watching you, too." Now the more I watch my fellowman, the more I see myself and how un-free we really are. But it also reminds me to love my fellowman. Dad and Mom had such balance in the structure of their lives. With all the unpleasantness around us, it seems like the hard times were nothing more than a step to the next day. It never was a question about who was the boss. The thing that mattered was getting the job done, and at the end of the day, everybody was happy.

No one ever had to wonder whether there was love between Dad and Mom; they always made it so clear. They would take walks in the fields, and into the woods, you could see him from way off, he would take a hand full of dirt and sift it through his hands. Seems like he would crush the dirt to feel the texture of the soil to see it was right for what ever he wanted to plant. Because whatever we planted always would do well. I often check the texture of my life to see if I need to work on myself, and see if I find any hardness, or things such as attitude, unkindness, selfishness, jealousy, judgmental, bitterness, hatred, bigotries, and all kinds of things that need crushing, that would keep me from growing and prevent me from becoming a better person and not hinder me from living a free life. One day a nearby neighbor— and nearby means a few miles down the road—asked Douglas, "You don't have to work dem boys that hard just to raise a crop, do ya?" He simply agreed and said, "I ain't raising no crop; I'm raising Men." When he finished the few rows, he would give the plow to us and go on to something else. There was always something that needed to be done. He had to continue sharpening the plow tools, fixing the wagon, mending the mules' collars, patching the house, making cotton sacks, cutting hoe handles or sharpening axes, and the list could go on for quite a long time. When he finished doing that, he would go somewhere to work for cash. There were always people needing someone to help them out. What we didn't understand was every chance he got to earn money was being saved to move his family away from that life of hard work and no pay. But he never had to concern himself about Fred and me taking care of the plowing and planting because he had already laid the foundation for what he expected us to follow. Now do you remember what we said at the beginning about the chain-of-command system? Fred was the one in authority when Dad was not there. I obeyed Fred as if he was Daddy in these kinds of situations.

"HARD WORK NEVER HURT ANYBODY"

Daddy was not a man that wanted to work us hard. He wanted us to work smarter than harder. His way of thinking was if we do it right the first time, there was no need of doing it over. For the most part, Dad's vocabulary consisted of about two words—right and wrong. Anything between was nothing but bull, and I truly believe that today.

Now please, you must understand when I said Dad plowed just a few rows and gave the plow to me and my brother, that didn't mean we just plowed a few rows. We had fields and acres to plow, about four or five times including the planting. We grew cotton, corn and peanuts; the plantation owners required this. But Dad would plant what was the better market item because he was still hoping it would give him some profit at harvest time—wrong.

As I take a look back in the rearview mirror of our lives, some might say they would make some drastic changes, if the opportunity would present itself, well I don't fit that particular category, and I think I can be a spokesman for the rest of the gang.

We were very well off, and that means even with the conditions as they were, having had the opportunity to live in that part of our nation's history. I see it as a blessing, and with all of the experiences in so many areas at such a young age, I think it was worth all of the negative stuff that was going on at the time, but there were so many positive things going on as well. I hope no one feel that I'm trying to gain any sympathy or seem as I deserve any kind of medal, I just felt I might have some experiences someone might find interesting about our country some sixty odd years ago.

We learned about how multiplicity this world is we live in, and how everything seems to just know how to live in pure harmony with each other except mankind. But as we were not allowed to associate with each other, that meant our Caucasian counterparts, we still had some real balance in our lives. As I think about it as far as freedom is concern maybe we had more freedom then than now, but we were taught more about love, morality, honesty, truth, respect, dignity, selflessness and that produces integrity, but once you lose the former which is "Love" then all of the rest is pretty much up for grabs.

I would like to see our society's value system change, and how could this happen? Then everybody knew everybody and when one was in need everybody was in need and when one hurts everybody hurts and that's when people cared for someone other than self.

Rev. Dr. Martin Luther King, Jr. said once, and I quote "As long as people are poverty stricken, nobody can be totally secure, and as long as there are millions of people in our world suffering with various diseases, nobody can be totally healthy."

We have become so disconnected from each other until nobody knows anybody anymore. This is the main cause of what I think is a great gulf we have made between us. Now we are drifting further apart and until we really start living the one nation, and united we stand, and all of the words that fits the particular occasion and become true neighbors as we suppose to be, we will never be a free nation, as we have been told we are.

With such a vast range of diversity to draw from, it seems as if this would be the right time to really enjoy the freedom that was made possible by our participation in so many ways to help others gain what we so freely enjoyed until now. I believe we have forgotten what we really have; maybe it would behoove all of us to re-visit our past. Maybe we would have a greater appreciation of where we are now and then better prepare for a more sound and healthy feature.

Now Daddy just knew what kind of dirt would be better for growing the best crops. We had different kinds of soils, there was Black dirt, and a sandy like mixed soil, clay and just plain dirt, and this probably doesn't mean anything to anybody, but every thing we did had a specific meaning, and has a more lasting value now. I think by being able to live free, I am able to see not only a true picture but a more clear one, for I have no regrets of my past, and the picture that's left with me is not a murky image of that life. Fred and I were talking about working, plowing, chopping, and picking cotton, pulling corn, chopping shaking and stacking peanuts, in the hot summer days, you could see the heat waves in front of us looked like water dancing in our faces, seemed like it was just out of our reach but it to just an illusion.

Forever working in the heat, our feet's backed from the sun parched earth, temperatures reaching above 100 degrees, this was every day except Sundays.

We would go to church every Sunday. These were always happy times because this is where everybody would meet after a long week of very hard work. If it sounds like my family was the only family working hard, let me tell you there were three kinds of work: hard, harder, and even more hard. Every family in the state worked all three of them. This was the example of that form of equality we shared; all blacks were treated equal.

See, equality has always been there for us. We all were treated equal, what I would hope for that equal rights be measured by equal justice, by the standards of the law. And I don't mean Jim Crow, either. Today when I hear the words equal rights, I have one of those flashbacks. The reason I say this is because first, I would like to know what or whom am I being equal to. We always had the law of equality on our side, and it was equally wrong. I often think when I see some of the more primitive and as they might say, uncivilized parts of the world, I can relate to that very well, and with hope one day their experiences will be living in more healthy surroundings and modern conditions. We as a nation have always tried to help other parts of the world, and we've made some hug contributions. But there is still quite a large spot of land here that needs taking care of.

Again, this word illusion, just keep presenting it self let's see what it means, and why I keep yakking about working so hard, and never ever received any compensation for our labor after gaining this as one of the benefits. Under the act of freedom yes, I think this is an illusion and I stand correction if I'm assuming something different from what I just stated, so yes, I see a picture of one thing but in reality it is something totally different. Illusion (1) "Something that deceives by producing a false or misleading impression of reality. (2) The state or condition of being deceived; misapprehension. (3) An instance of being deceived. (4) A perception, as of visual stimuli (optical illusion) that represents what is perceived in a way different from the way it is in reality.

In the past few decades or so, when the word illusion comes up in conversation, the one name that's usually up front is Mr. David Copperfield, a master magician and a very popular illusionist.

After many years, months, days, and hours of practicing, this gentleman has the ability of pulling rabbits out of top hats, slice beautiful women in half, or make things disappear and reappear, people, places and things. And some of the things are very big things but he's never lost anybody or anything yet. He always brings them back. Over the years he has collected props and used numerous techniques to create all kinds of illusions. With the slight of hand, his art has become seamless. It's quite believable to the eye. I've watched his performance on TV many times, and I've found myself not wanting to believe it's only an illusion. He has done some pretty awesome things, but he always returns things right back as they were.

I've only seen him perform on TV, but I sure would like to see him in person. His skills are nothing short of amazing; his deceptive slight of hand is absolutely mind-boggling. His skills keep his audience completely mesmerized and spellbound.

But when you take a good look at it, I guess these two professions are about the same. Our elected official keeps their audiences, we, the citizens, mesmerized the same way as do Mr. Copperfield and his audiences. It's amazing to see how we are all trapped in a make believe world audience, and watching our daily lives being mutilated with the same form of illusionary trickery.

The life of a farmer should be a good life because the importance of this industry is to keep the food supply plentiful at all times, with every kind of food for the entire world. And that's a lots of food, but year after year somehow it's always there, in abundance. I know I'm the only one who knows these things—yea, right—but the conditions should have been much better not just for the farmers, but for every aspect of life/ My reason for talking about the farm life is because that's the part of my life that I hold so many memories of. It brought to my thinking, after the Israelites was brought out of the land of Egypt, was there ever a thought or even a yearning to revisit that brutal and bitter life? It still amazes me to see how we as peoples can always go back to what we know. It doesn't matter how horrible it might have been, the truth is we always find it easier to go back or hold on to our past rather than grab a chunk of faith and claim the preciousness that the future holds. And please don't think there well be no difficultness, but if we've really learned from our past those experiences will help make things more enjoyable. One way I've learned is to re-shape some of my thinking is I use the approach to not problems, but projects and address them from that aspect, then prioritize my projects, by managing that specific project.

We had some very good times, learning how so many different things together can produce so many great things.

Something like that ole jigsaw puzzle, or maybe for a better word the picture puzzle. There are so many pieces some look almost identical but there's a big difference in each of them. But if you just be patient and find the right piece and carefully place it in the right place, soon you will see the true picture being manifest before your eyes. Now you didn't create that picture, you just developed it, and then you can display it and then it can be enjoyed by many, such as if we learn to live a free life, then others might have had some puzzle like pieces in their lives and not yet figured out what piece goes where.

Mom was a very good cook. I used to watch her preparing to make a cake or pies or soups and stews. She would get all of the ingredients and place them on the table. We had no counters then. She would measure all the ingredients first and then she would incorporate them together and let them join the heat treatment process for awhile. Then you can really appreciate how well things work together, but we would all get to taste it even before it was ready, because we would sop the pan and lick the spoon. We started to understand the great benefits in living in a multiplicity society as it is.

There was so much diversity all around us. We could understand the great benefits in having these many things by incorporating each other's ideas, time, resources, experiences and "yes" criticisms, just as the ingredients and the outcome of Mom's cooking.

Mom and all the other women had a scrap bag where they kept all kinds of scrap cloth of all colors and sizes. They would keep this material until they had enough to make a quilt, and then all the women would come together and help each other. They took four strands of haywire equal in length and hung each strand from the ceiling of the house. They would connect the ends of the wire to two size boards. They would place a thin material to the frames; this would be the base of the quilt. Then they would begin with all the different cloth and they would sew and spit, most of them dipped snuff, but what great times they had helping each other. And they did this until each of them had a quilt made. They were made with all different material, of all shapes, sizes, and colors, but the finished product was sensational.

The "wild kingdom" it is sometimes called. All kinds of animals, fowls, fish, trees, flowers and yes people, all over the place, all existing together. So I hope you see what I mean.

Well, it's time for us to move to another house, which was seventy-five acres of land. It was supposed to belong to my daddy, but he was told later that the records were read wrong. My daddy was devastated, but once again, there was nobody to appeal to.

I think the reason life deals us so many different hands so to speak, is it makes us become better players when we sit down at the table of life. By the time I had reached school age, we had already learned quite a bit from being put into so many situations where the availability's of choices wasn't there, and to say I didn't want to, but that was not an option. So we had to sink or swim, and swim we did.

Daddy had almost enough money for train fair, and when

I say almost, I mean within a year or so. Now our farming was coming to an end. After a record-breaking harvest, Mr. Ben Garrett, this was our landowner who went to receive the profits, told Daddy, "You and your kids did well this time," and gave daddy twelve dollars. That's the first time I saw my Daddy in tears, he kept repeating "But my children they worked so hard," and that's when I am sure in his mind "the green flag has dropped."

As I think about it now, I realize what motivated Dad to get us out of that place. It wasn't so much of not getting paid, because we never did, anyway. But when Mr. Garrett gave him twelve dollars for a whole year's pay for he and his children; that's when he finally said "that's enough." This was in 1948. Another landowner lived a few miles from us. He came to Daddy and said, "I was told you and your children sometimes work away from home." Daddy said, "Sometimes." I don't think Daddy knew this man very well. He told Daddy if he would help him, he would pay more than the going wages. Daddy said it would be about two to three weeks, and the man was very disappointed. See, this was right in the midst of our season. He needed this done like yesterday, and he said "Well I will lose everything," and daddy asked what did he have that needed to be picked that soon? He said velvet beans, and Dad said, "Just a minute, sir. We will help you." Daddy knew what this man would have lost. These beans were black with fiberglass-like fur, and when it got on your skin, it felt like fiberglass. He said it would take us a week, but Dad said no because he had his own crops to farm. We went the next morning very early, and we finished in about three days. This man was very pleased, and Daddy was glad, too, because in another week they would have been gone. The urgency of this particular bean was after it gets ripe it would spoil on the vine real quick. It's a bean that was used for some kind of oil, and it was not edible. He paid Daddy more than he first said, and all of us got a crisp five-dollar bill.

I just knew I was the richest person in the world. It wasn't Mr. Gates's time yet, but in comparison I thought my name was like "Mr. Gates." (Hope you don't mind, sir). We moved to this other place in late part of 1948 after all the crops were gathered, and our farming days were over.

Fred started working at the lumber mill just outside of town. This is when he realized there was another side of life other than the farm. This was a time all of us had to readjust to not having to work in the hot sun all day. Ethel and I would begin our day at four a.m. We got breakfast for the entire family because Daddy and Fred started work at six a.m. From that time on we were washing dishes, making our beds, and getting ready for school. After school Ed and my jobs were keeping wood cut for heating the house, washing cloths, and cooking.

Wood was the main source of energy; the fuel that kept things going. Keeping the yard swept was another part of our chores. Instead of having a lawn, we had to chop the grass with a hoe and keep the yard smooth and clean. This was done about once a week.

Fred bought his first car, and we didn't quite understand how he did that with the money he was earning. Things were really going swell until one day, Mom sent me to someone's house in the car for something. The police stopped me and had me to drive back home and park the car. Then they proceeded to take me to jail for driving without a license. Mom told them her husband was working at Burgeon's Lumber Mill, and they should let him know they had his son in jail.

Well he didn't do so, but cousin Allie saw them and came to our house and mom told him they had taken me to jail, well he went to the mill and told Daddy, and after not very long Mr. Burgeons and daddy came to the jail. Mr. Burgeons stormed straight to the judge and said, "What do these police mean taking this boy from his home? His daddy works for me, and I am losing time here with this nonsense. You better let that boy out and I mean right now."

So the judge said, "I'm very sorry, and it won't happen again." Well, that's the way that system worked then and no doubt even now. The thing about me driving was not at all uncommon, because most of the boys were driving at seven or eight years old. That was a part of our daily jobs, anyway. But I left with nothing on my record. In the early spring of 1949, one of Daddy's brothers drove from Chicago. He had a new 1949 Lincoln. Every time he drove it around anywhere, he would get stopped by the police just because he had a new car, but nothing ever happened. Today in some places, and not only in the South, that kind of harassment still goes on.

It's Mom's time again: November 24, 1950, and another girl, Lillian Faye.

That is it. Daddy was about 44 years old. I can't imagine what was going through his head. With no education and not much money and no job, he was taking his family to Chicago. Oh yeah, Rosie lee was in Ohio and married; Laura was already in Chicago. The only thing he had done was farm all of his life.

But we were taught as long as we had God and each other, it was all we needed.

Everywhere we went, people asked when we were leaving and what we'd do in a big city like Chicago. Well, we didn't know, seeing as we'd never been there before. But we knew as long as Daddy said it was ok, then, it was ok.

This was the time for the very thing Daddy had been teaching us all those years about faith and how to put it to the test. I am sure he was well aware of what he was doing. As for Mom, she was more than ready. Now Dad was not about to take his family halfway across the country and didn't think about the consciences he might face. But he knew that God had taken care of him all these years, and He wasn't about to stop now. So he took Mom and the four young girls, and off to the Windy City they went, leaving Fred, Ed, and me to join them latter.

Now here was something we'd never expected. All the rest of the family I knew had just left and Fred was quite competent and responsible so that was ok, but we had never been separated before. But we knew as long as we stayed tougher we would be fine, and cousin Allie was very near to help us. For whatever reason we had to stay, it was just for a few weeks. But nonetheless I think this is when I learned how to pray, and my fears seemed to just vanish. Am I suggesting prayer? Absolutely. Now, as I stand on the sixty-fifth mile mark on the highway of my life, I take regular look backs to see where I've come from and how I've gotten this for. I can say with 100% certainty that having a loving family who loved the Lord, and who loved all people without having a reason to, not looking at anybody expecting to see anyone except our self, and being ready to help whenever the need was taught all nine of us to never quit. They told us you might give out, but don't give up, and always pray for ourselves and others.

Because if we had not utilized prayer and the positive results it provided, I don't think the road we've travel would have been as joyful as it has been, and I mean in abundance.

After spending twelve years of my life on a farm, the time has come not to forget the farm life but rather utilize the things I learned there.

In the late fall of 1950, I guess this was the happiest day of my life. It was the night before we left. Sleeping was out of the question. Fred was the perfect parent at the time, because he was the oldest and he was the one in charge.

I often reflect and remember where he got his training.

He made sure Ed and I were as comfortable as possible. Wednesday morning at 7:00 a.m., Cousin Allie drove us to the train station for a 10:00 a.m. departure. I remember standing on the platform, gazing down the tracks, looking for the train, seem like it took forever for it to arrive, but after awhile the conductor asked the boys, "Where ye going?" And Fred said, "Sir, we are going to Chicago." He said, "Where's your ma and pa?" Again Fred said, they were already there, and about then he said, "All right boys, hear she comes, and you boys' taker easy." "Yesser," was our reply. I later learned that out final destination was Colvert, Michigan.

There were plenty mixed feelings; we were leaving behind the only life we new, all we had ever done, and all the people we'd known. We were going somewhere very far away, but having not seen the rest of the family for almost a month as this was the first time we had ever been separated, just to get to them, that's all that mattered. We said our last goodbyes and boarded the train. Of course there were seating arrangements, meaning we were in the colored section. But by that time we were well aware of that, which was just another day.

After a sleepless Tuesday night before, I soon gave in to a long nap. When I woke up, that's when things started to become real. I don't know whether I was glad to leave the only life I'd known or just excited to be rejoined with the family. As daylight started to vanish into the night, my face pressed against the window, looking out into the darkness only catching a glimpse of myself in the window from a quick reflection of light on the train. There were many thoughts in my little head, and I was wondering what it would be like when we reached Chicago.

It's human nature for us to return to the past and what we know. It matters not how horrible it might have been, rather than go forward to the unknown, isn't it? I think Fred must have known, or maybe he was thinking the same things. It seemed like it took forever to get there, but it was only about five days as I recall. As we passed through so many towns, things got pretty interesting. I began to see there was more to this world other than the farm in Georgia, but we had never seen it before. The only other places were in our geography books. This was a new beginning to open doors we never knew existed.

When I awakened from a long sleep, the first thing I remember seeing was the huge buildings. I had never seen anything like this before.

After what seemed like a very long trip on the train, we heard the conductor coming through the train cars announcing all the towns and finally, after what seemed like forever, "Union Station, Chicago."

We got off the train and took a taxi to Aunt Brownie's house. She lived at 3702 South Parkway, which is now Dr. Martin Luther King Dr. A very interesting sight along the streets was all of the terrific lights. It seemed like there were more people in one area than there were in the whole town of Cuthbert. She lived on the third floor in an apartment building. That was very different from those wooden houses I had become so comfortable in.

We stayed there until Sunday morning. My cousin Laura Ann took Ed and me for a short sightseeing trip. I never thought so much was even in the world; just being there was enough. Indoor plumbing and hot water coming out of the faucets. Bathtubs, television sets they were called, even lights coming on with a wall switch. Then the movies, and to see there were no seating regulation was another learning experience. The next week we took the Greyhound bus to Colvert, Michigan, where we rejoined the family. But here is where it gets really interesting.

When Daddy came to pick us up, it was nearly dark. The bus stopped on the road near the house, what a bummer, it was another farm, and I thought Dad brought us all this way just to start the same ole thing over again.

This brings to mind another story I heard a long time ago. I like good stories. They seem to just put you in that place. This one is about being critical of the decisions of others and judging from a distance.

A man was hunting one day, and he came to the top of a hill, and saw a man being chased by a bull. He would run into a cave, and in the cave he would go, and as soon as he entered the cave he would run out again. The bull would charge after him, and again he ran to a near by tree, and up the tree he went, and right back down again, and after this was repeated several times, the hunter decided to help this poor dumb and many other names for this man. He raised his gun and shot a few rounds and chased the bull away, finally he approached the exhausted man and very harshly inquired, please tell me, why wouldn't you just stay in the cave? Well you couldn't see from where you were, there's a bear in that cave, ok replied the hunter and why didn't you stay in the tree? Again sir from where you were, you couldn't see as I did, that tree is full of poise ness snakes, so from where I was I was using what seemed to work.

The deal was, Daddy's half brother had a very large farm there, and he needed help for a while. Dad would be closer to Chicago, and when he found work, we would move. After checking this situation and realizing what was happening, we got all right. But I am glad we did because it wouldn't have mattered anyway. But like the man and the hunter, we only saw one part of the picture from where we were. Daddy was using that farm only to get where he wanted to go, and all was well.

But the difference was, they grew fruits: grapes, pears, apples, peaches, and blueberries. They also grew veggies: potatoes, greens, beans, and tomatoes. They had six cows, two horses, and many chickens, so we had no problem adjusting. In fact, it was an advantage having prior experience.

We were anxious to explore this new life, but the main thing was we were all back together. We had been separated for almost a month.

But this illusion of being free kept following us. Uncle Jessie and Aunt Georgia, with that name alone should have told us something. But just leaving the state of Georgia, and all its missing links, I thought this would be a piece of cake—wrong. Aunt Georgia wore all the pants, so to speak.

She was the next of kin to Satan himself. She was very "religious," and her way was the only way. The first thing we had to attend was her church, which was one that our parents didn't really approve of. But we still had the upper hand because we still knew how to live free in the midst of confusion. Now our teaching was really put to the test. The Georgia girl was the very image of evil. She saw nothing worthwhile in us. But what we had learned long before, how to handle certain situations and knowing how to respond to them, sure was helpful. They would always say hold on to what you have because someday you will have a need for it. Now this was the time.

It's been said, "It's better to have it and not need it than need it and not have it." We sure needed it. She had a new bunch of names for us, and most of them were not at all good. But Mom would keep all of us under close watch in case she had to step in and keep Aunt Georgia at bay. Trust me, she was quite capable of doing that. The boys were better off than the girls, and we never knew why.

Daddy was working anywhere he could find work. It was just like back home. He was able to keep quit busy because there was not too much he couldn't do. We missed most of that school year, getting transferred in the mid-term. There were new waves of problems. This was the first time we experienced integration. This was something within itself. We were put back a grade. They said the children from the South were not as smart as the Northern children. So to Aunt Georgia, this confirmed what she had said when she first saw us. Her favorite name was "dumb bunnies."

This was a very new and different kind of dealing. Back in the old country, we all spoke Georgian, both the whites and the blacks. But these teachers and students both kept us at the long end of the stick because we had that Southern twang in our speech. The few blacks that attended the school had a social image to protect. Now remember, back in the old country, the whites had to help the blacks under the cover of secrecy or they would be labeled as "nigger lovers." What a label. Now here was a new twist, learning how to handle being outcast by both the blacks and the whites. I think that was a very good lesson for me. I'm to always remember I must have compassion for others.

These are some of the things that happened to us that we had never experienced before. Being discriminated by people who looked like us. It seemed as if we were living between two different times rather than two different places. But now I can appreciate what that experience taught me. I see the real picture of discrimination, and it isn't just the whites discriminating against the blacks. You can be discriminated by those within your own race. This was a blessing for us. It let us know you don't have to be any certain race, religion, gender, or whatever your preference, or choices may or may not be. As long as we are in this human form, we are quite capable of possessing these horrible evils.

But we were ready and well prepared to play whatever hand we were dealt.

One of my teachers told the principal she could not teach a student that was retarded, and I couldn't speak English. Well, this caused Daddy to make a visit to the school. They sent me to a speech class for three sessions. After the sessions were over, they determined I had a 100% Southern ascent, and nothing could be done about that. I would soon grow out of it. But fifty-some years later, it's just as it was the day I left. I wondered if there was a place where I could fit in. In gym it was discovered that my athleticism was not very good, and I am being quite modest. I had very good sports skills. Then things started to ease somewhat.

I remember having two pairs of pants, one coat, and two shirts, but Mom required that we be clean every day. That meant coming home every day to wash and iron our clothes and get ready for the next day. This lasted for the time we stayed there. This stop was temporary until Daddy found a job in Chicago.

Soon could not be soon enough. What we had to do was continue applying what we had been taught earlier, love even when conditions that's around you say different.

Back in Georgia we saw just one side of prejudice. Well I know, this is the first time the real truth about this have ever been revealed but after awhile you will see this thing I keep referring to as an optical illusion.

Our fears are our captors.

The things we fear are the very things that control us and prevent us from living a free life. In our case, it was the law.

The laws were meant to keep a balance and help to protect the liberties of all people.

The Constitution of the United States of America

"We the people of the United States, in order to form a more perfect union, establish justice, ensure domestic tranquility provide for the common defense promote the general welfare and secure the blessings of liberty to ourselves and our posterity, do ordain and establish this Constitution for the United States of America."

Here again, why does this freedom keep poppin' up and cause all of us to feel so helpless? It's hard for me to understand how we can claim to be free when we are living in constant fear.

Fear a Superficial Reality

President Roosevelt said, "All you have to fear is fear itself."

Fear is a big part of our lives. There's plenty of it around, and it's been here for quite sometime. It looks like it will be with us for quite awhile.

Webster brakes it down this way—"a distressing emotion arouse by impending danger, evil, pain, etc, whether the threat is real or imagined: the feeling or condition of being afraid in a specific instance or propensity for such a feeling: a fear of heights concern: solicitude: a fear for someone's safety: reverential awe something that causes fright or apprehension. To have reverential awe of archaic is to experience fear in oneself." This force has been a part of our lives from day one, so we should know how to deal with it by now. It is one of the biggest intangibles that keeps us from living a more free and complete life. Here in America, we keep saying things like "united we stand" and "one nation under God." But if you take a look at when those statement are made, you'll find only when we are facing some kind of difficult situation that threatens our little comfort zone is the only time these statement are used. As soon as the threat passes, we revert back to that same form of individualism, only to find the same fears of being alone are still present. I remember on the farm, all the chickens would be out in the yard scratching and pecking. Suddenly a hawk would appear you know that old saying? "Out of nowhere," never see them looking up, but they just knew when there was danger or the threat near, all of them would head for cover. Then as soon as the threat leave, they would always return back to their scratching and pecking. The thing about that Southern non-freedom; you always knew exactly where you stood. It was told to us, "When you pass the Mason-Dixon Line, you're ok; but in reality, we never knew when we crossed that line.

Remember the frog eggs? Yes, we are one nation, and yes, we are under God. But if we don't stand united when there are no immediate threats, then we will not stand when that danger finally arrive. As long as that embryo stays intact, the eggs will survive until they mature to the tadpole stage.

In a free society as we are, or as we think we are, our fears keep pushing us further apart and the further apart we become, our behavior starts to change and the manner of conduction oneself responsible, or irresponsible, will begin. The psycho, animal-like behavior will become observable in human or animal fashion; thus the aggregate response to internal and external stimuli that stereotypes different groups, the action or reaction that is found under any given circumstance. But is this a good reason to continue down that same old path? I think not. But the picture that keeps presenting itself to me as being a free people is just an illusion.

Knowing where we came from and where we are today, I truly believe the real freedom comes by choice and not by proclamation. When we were declared free by proclamation in 1865, did anything change? No. History tells us most of the slaves continued serving their masters the same way they did before. So maybe they had learned how to live free before they were given that so-called freedom.

If anyone can give us freedom, it can be taken back. But if we learn to live free, then no one can ever take it away. Even more importantly, the ones that think they are giving us freedom are in fact not free themselves. I believe our lawmakers and those who have been given the responsibility of enforcing it are more insecure than any of us. They need to feel like they are the only ones who know anything about anything. I believe they are really bound and don't have a clue about being free. Somewhere along the way, someone told them that money could fix everything. But we as a nation are now in greater financial difficulty. I don't think they have a clue or an idea of recovering. What is wrong with this? They want everybody to feel the presence of being enslaved spiritually, mentally, economically, socially, and politically.

Living on the farm we were in fact free, but the fears had been handed down from generation to generations, and with every generation they become like big trees, each feet it grows up it grows down twice as much, until it's enough root to withstand such encounters that lies ahead. All tall buildings, such as the Sears Tower and the John Hancock Buildings, are built to withstand different adversities such as strong winds, earthquakes, and so on. The higher you go up, the deeper you must dig down so the foundation will be on solid rock.

We learned very early the foundation of our faith was in the Lord Jesus Christ.

Remember what fear means? "Some distressing emotions aroused by impending danger, evil, or pain, etc., whether the threat is real or imagined." So what I see, we're all afraid of discovering how much we are alike and not how different we are.

I started to see that after we moved from Georgia because there we was not allowed to associate with one another than (our kind so to speak) so we really never had the chance to learn about others' likeness or differences. When we moved, this gave me the opportunity to make some new discoveries. Much to my surprise, I found there was no real difference in any of us. But I keep seeing we the people family, but we the people, find it rather difficult to accept each other on the basis of just plain human beings.

If the old and the young, the rich and poor, and each other ethnic groups, educated, and those that are not, short tall and every other distinction of people, claim total separation from each other we would be totally lost. But this is exactly where I see we're headed. Once again, I find all the ways we find to categorize ourselves leaves me with the impression that we are afraid of discovering there are no differences in any of us. But by doing so, it gives us a false since of security. By measures of possessions and education, what school they attended, the size of their bank accounts, or whether they live in a mansion or run-down shack, we're all one people whether we like it or not.

I was born on a farm in the backwoods of Georgia, but until 1950 when we moved to Chicago, I'd never turned on a light switch before, and I'd never used indoor plumbing. When I moved to Michigan, I'd never seen schoolbooks with all the pages until then. I'd never ridden anywhere on public transportation other than the back seats in the back of the bus. When we boarded the school bus in Michigan, my first impulse was to go to the back of the bus. You see, the wells of segregation and intimidation had long been dug deep in the fields of our forefathers' mines. So the legacy was quite prevalent in the lives of their descendants. But even by being taught how to live free, there still were boundaries. When I arrived at school the first day, the first thing I wanted to know was, where was our washroom? Not just the boys' washroom, but the washroom for the colored boys.

These were the laws that impregnated the minds and souls of a race of people and gave birth that left a cold and bitter legacy that was passed on to us.

The clouds of racism and separatism still hang heavy over the heads of America today, and most people still do not see we have a major problem.

Daddy, with the help of Uncle Jessie, got a job with a meat company's packinghouse. Stockyards were quite popular in Chicago in those days, and soon after, he got an apartment at 6814 S. Perry. We moved in during the summer break of 1953.

We lived in a community with only a few black families at the time, and it was just fine.

The late great track star Jessie Owens and his family lived only a few streets from where we lived, and across the street from us was the Dysen family. Lonnie and Marvin, we were good friends all through our earlier school years. After their schooling, both of them went into the radio broadcasting business. Marvin later became the general manager for one of Chicago's largest radio stations, WGCI FM. My first none black friend's name was Bobbie Diaz and his family. It was a community that resembled what I think a community should be like today. It was a very racially diverse and close-knit neighborhood that had the same concern of all of its members. Mom was always a homemaker, and when we became known, our house was the place all the children would come after school. The working parents knew they would be ok. Things were much different then, but this is the way we lived back in Georgia. Everybody looked after everybody. The only difference was people of all races were living and working tougher. Our favorite hangout was a small soda fountain next to a drugstore on the corner of Wentworth and 69th street. Right down the street on Wentworth, the legendary guitarists and blues singer Jimmy Reed had an apartment on the second floor. It was quite a mixed culture in a small community. An automobile dealer was on the corner of Perry and 69th Street. They kept the lights on in the lot so we could play ball after dark. There was a small neighborhood grocery store on the opposite corner; Chuck was the owner's name. He was a very kind man. What was going on in my mind was the difference living in Georgia and living in Chicago. I didn't see anything we had done differently, but things sure were much different.

I attended Parker Elementary School. I was the only black student in most of my classes as for that I was one of a very few black students in the entire school and it was never a problem. Soon after, new neighbors moved in next door to us. They were two sisters. One had four children—three boys and one girl. One of the boys was my age. His name was Richard Goodman. He and I became very good friends. This was when my life started to change, and that change has lasted until this day. Although we haven't seen each other in quite some time, I can say with all certainty that we still are friends. We were like twins. There was hardly a time when you would see one of us without the other. To my mother he was like another son, and to his mother I was like another son. We ran track together and won many events. Shooting marbles was quit a popular thing for young boys. We were playing AA class baseball, but to me that was like playing professional ball in comparison with what I played back home.

Playing on a baseball diamond with real uniforms with numbers and the uniforms was the same as my teammates, using baseballs and gloves that wasn't made by Daddy, with real umpires officiating the games, you couldn't have told me this wasn't the majors. I never got that far but coming from playing in the cow-pastures in Georgia and playing in Washington park in Chicago, on a real baseball diamond, I feel just like I made it. Richard never played baseball as much as I did, and he never acquired the real love for it like I did. I remember one day we were practicing for the next day's game, someone popped up a very high fly ball and Richard got under the ball to make the catch. The ball went right through the web of the glove and almost knocked his eye out. The best thing about that, we were right across the street from the hospital. But when my friend got hit, I forgot all about that game. My friend was hurt, and that was the only thing important to me.

I know I had the ability to play at the major league level, but I just didn't have the physical stature that was needed. But I'm well satisfied with what my life has been up to this point.

Having a television, we could see Jackie Robinson playing. The tension had subsided quite a bit since he first entered in 1947, which was a major breakthrough. That in itself was just another way to make sure everything remained the same.

Before we could only hear the ballgames on radio. Sometimes the reception was not very clear. Now here we are in 1953, there were quite an addition to the rosters by incoming black players and don't think it was just because the mindset was changing. There was a great financial benefit for the owners and these newly discovered athletes earning their rightful place. I was there when two of my favorite black players were signed with the Chicago Cubs, Mr. Cub himself, Ernie Banks and Gene Baker. By this time the major leagues were full throttle with, as they said then, the "colored boys." But the biggest news around the baseball games was between Mickey Mantle and Willie Mayes. Now they weren't talking about their ability. Both were great baseball players. The noise was, should a black man earn as much money as a white man? Well, here we are again. I think that's one of the questions still being asked today from the sports to the corporate levels and in all other areas of this free society.

Now Richard and I became like inseparable friends over the years. We did almost everything together, all through school.

Daddy was so happy he had a job that he could support his family. He worked the 2nd shift, from 3:00 pm till 11:00 pm, and he was earning about $60.00 a week, about average for stockyard labor or any other laborer. That was the only thing Dad was qualified to do, and many other black men, but they never thought they were capable of doing anything else because that's what they've been told all of their lives.

After school, I would go to the A&P grocery store with a Radio Flyer wagon and carry people's groceries home. I would make five or ten dollars most weeks, and that was pretty good and it helped out at home too. My good friend Chuck Scott, who was a "Caucasian" boy, would come home with me for lunch almost every day. The reason I keep using words like Caucasian and black is because this was very different from what I had experienced in my earlier years. Fred was now working at the (CBA) Chicago Bar Association as a dishwasher and buss boy. Laura was working there also and had been for quite sometime. She helped him get hired. She had been given the position as a hostess, and that alone was pretty big stuff. They had never had a black hostess before, so that went well. Ethel Lee (Gee) became very ill and after a visit to Cook County hospital, they diagnosed her as having diabetes. Now this was something we were not at all ready to hear, but as always, unless it's something we want we are never ready. Cook County was where people would go without insurance coverage and/or not having the ability to pay, and as far as I know it's still that way. The diabetic food was very expensive but that's what had to be done, that became top priority. And with Daddy making so little money and Fred's very little, things still was very tight, I asked Daddy if I could drop out of school and take a job to help out. Well, that didn't go over so well. He said the Lord would take care of it all. And soon after that Aunt Bownie's husband, John, but we called him Uncle Sunny, he was a butcher in a predominantly, and that was with very few exceptions, Jewish community grocery store. I came home from school and he had left word for me to call him at the store. I call and talked to the owner Al Miller, and his wife Esther, and they wanted me to come in. They needed a delivery boy and after I told Dad what they wanted he said "Okay," as long as I kept my grades up it would be fine. The store was located at 806 E. 53rd St. and low and behold they started paying me $20.00 a week. Now remember this is the first time I even seen money since that $5.00 Daddy paid me for picking those velvet beans, in fact I thought money had been abolished since then. Now, "Mr. Gates, the competition would have really been on." I really felt like this was the land of promise, I told Mom after a couple of paydays, which was every Saturday, I want to take care of the biggest household bills other than the rent which then was a furniture bill. Mom said that would be a big responsibility and she would have to ask Daddy and a couple of days passed and she said, "Your daddy said he would speak to you when he come home tonight," and about eleven thirty when he arrived, he came in and got me out of bed. He said, "What's this about you wanting to help me with paying these bills?" with a smile on his face. "Yes Sir, Daddy," I said, "I am a man now and I want to have some responsibilities, as a man." And with such fury in his face, he said, "Don't you ever let me hear you say you're a man again." I was completely floored, then he put his hands on my head and said, "Daddy want you to just be a man, and when you be a man you will never have to say you're a man." And then he put his arms around me and said, "Yes son you can help Daddy."

All of the people were very kind and generous to me. The tips were more than my pay. It took some explaining from Mr. Miller and Uncle Sunny to convince me I was to keep the tips; this was a complete new word to me. Mr. Miller took me and explained how this new system I had discovered really worked. I would bring all of the money and give it to him or his wife. Al got Uncle Sunny and told him to help explain that this money didn't belong to the store.

After my new discovery, paying that bill would be a breeze.

At first Daddy wasn't completely sure about all the tips I was bringing home. One day I went to work right after school and Al and his wife Esther, was telling me how nice of a Dad I had. I thanked them and went and asked Uncle Sonny, and he said, "Your Daddy just wanted to see where you worked, and how you was doing. Everything is okay he just wanted to check on you." I think this tip thing I had discovered kind of surprised Daddy as well as myself, but all went well. But this is what we as parents and guardians and friends neighbors should do, if anything seem out of the ordinary, then we should check it out, and that's what Dad was doing. Thanks Dad. These peoples were so kind to me. I didn't understand what I was doing to receive this much nice treatment from everybody. They made me feel like I was a part of that community, if only through working they made me feel like belonging outside of home and I am sure now they knew how our former lives had so many similarities. It's been said "everybody sees the same people at least twice in a lifetime." And I wonder if this was the second time for me as a descendant from the very early past. I remember many of them with numbers tattooed on their arms and some on the back of their hands. I first asked Uncle Sonny, and he said it was from something very bad that had happened to them a long time ago.

But my curiosity would not let me rest with just that. I knew one man who was very knowledgeable about lots of different stuff. I asked him. Mr. Hodges was his name. He was a black gentleman. When he told me the past history of those peoples, I thought about my grandparents and all of the other black families throughout this country. Then I felt a spiritual connection to a people who knew just what living a life of constant torture that will remain with you until this life ends; so perhaps that was explaining my feeling of belonging.

I was asked to do other favors such as wash windows. They were willing to pay me, and I was willing to do whatever I was asked. They were doing these things to help me, but they knew it was going to help my family. For Christmas, they really helped with monetary gifts. They were more than fair and quite liberal with their giving. Some of the envelopes were pretty heavy, and I know it was their way of being helpful, knowing we were in great need.

There was another family I have very fond memories of. A husband, wife and two boys, maybe twins, if not it seems like about a year difference in age. Their names was Mr. And Mrs. Gumble and their boys name were Greg and Brian. Mr. Gumble was an attorney who was a very well-respected and liked man in that community.

It seemed like there was always someone with whom I could find pleasure just being around; people that would give you encouraging words and good advice just like home. These men would have only one purpose in mind, and that was to make sure we were doing good in school and staying out of trouble. It seems like there were always people watching out for the young people. This is what a mentor was all about, and I really looked up to this gentleman. He never took me to a ballgame or movie or anything of this kind, but he just had the concern for others. He always had something very positive and meaningful to say to me. He encouraged me to stay in school and study hard to become a leader. Even speaking a language that seems like it's forgotten, like always tell the truth, be kind to people, help others when they need it, you know the same as Daddy had told us from birth. I learned very early after getting off the Greyhound bus in Colvert, Michigan, things was the same in the north as they were in the south, and this picture that presented itself was really an illusion. It seemed to be enlarging, but the road ahead didn't seem as rocky as the one behind, oh was I ever so wrong! But now I have gained some experience in different areas, but the best thing I have still is the know how to love and the willingness to use it. The choice was then, and it is today, to use love to combat all kind of situations, and guess what? It still works.

Now here comes something that has never been said before.

OK, I knew that wouldn't work. The reason hindsight is 20/20 is because we see where we've been, if we could see where we're going, then we would not have a future. But this is the value of history, it helps us prepare for the future and if we fail or refuse to watch and learn from our history, then our future is pretty much shot. I guess that's what it means, "there are great blessings in every lesson" and I can say, "No!" I do say, my past lessons have been nothing shorter than many great blessings.

I worked for the Millers for about a year. Al died suddenly and shortly after Ester sold the store. Another Jewish family bought the store. Their names were Abe and Ida Goldstein. They had a son named Larry and Mrs. Miller told them they was paying me twenty-five dollars a week, and you can see how unhappy that must of made me. That next Saturday they gave me a five dollar raise, but with a stipulation. I was not going to get the raise but when they took their money to the bank, they opened an account for me, with my raise. Now this was the bee's knee. (This little expression been with me for a long time.) I had something that none of my family members had at that time—a bank account.

As time passed, Jackie Robinson was almost accepted as a great ballplayer after dealing with so much rejection from his teammates, the fans, the media and all who were not of the colored race. We had heard about him on radio back in Georgia when he first signed with the Brooklyn Dodgers. But see him play and understand what he went through, and to say I understand, that's exactly what I mean.

Now we could finally see him play. Surely that was really great, but coming from Georgia, it was nothing new. It's the same story, just in another book.

The buzzing of Joe Louis's loss to Ezzard Charles some

years earlier had not yet silenced. The old retired men was good for keeping old stories alive and old events current but yet able to make them interesting. You could learn so much from those who had lived longer and were from different parts of the country, but their stories were so similar. Somehow we all had some of the same or very similar experiences. Most of them weren't that good. You could find them at most barbershops, playing checkers with self-made checkerboards, made of pieces from cardboard boxes. For the pieces they used Coca Cola tops. These old gents seemed to have found freedom through just talking about their sorrows. Like having a nagging thorn in the flesh, it can give you fits until it festers to form pus; generate purulent matter; suppurate; a festering wound. After it breaks and releases the pus, you soon forget about how bad the pain was. You just enjoy the new feeling.

General Dwight D. Eisenhower was coming up as the Republican candidate for president of the United States. But the black citizens were just becoming a part of that process. But we were still a free people, I thought; or was what we had been given an illusion?

We do have a democratic government, meaning, "pertaining to or characterized by political or social equality." The trouble with our system is the elected ones do not have the interest of the people in mind, rather the interest of particularly party or large business affiliations. Which totally violates the action of a democracy such as we are suppose to have, "a government by the people a form of government in which the supreme power is vested in the people, and exercised directly by them or by their elected agents, under a free electoral system." Now where is that freedom? Or is this kind of freedom for all the people? Or is this freedom just an illusion?

"The loudest sound of all is the sound of silence," and what I hear is a loud noise of absolute silence and apathy; a muffled voice of a frightened people. The fact that fear has such an impact on humanity can be used to starve any particular purpose at any given time, and no one can be blamed. I remember back in Georgia, if a fox or hawk was near the chickens, all of them would let it be known. If a snake's in the barn where the mules were they would kick their way out and run away, to where? It didn't matter; they just ran because they were afraid. Sometimes they would cause more damage by running than if they had just staid. So we know this fear is here to stay, but there's a better way to confront it.

When a society becomes frozen in its fears, then the process begins with making certain changes in the laws. I think that's exactly where we are today. But everybody keeps talking about how free we are and still living under the clouds of fear.

This was a very crucial time in our nation's history. Americans were returning home from Europe and Korea. The presence of military uniforms was everywhere. There was lots of laughter, joy, and happiness, but racial boundaries were still in place. Out of all the wars this country ever fought in and helped other countries, it's the same ole story here at home. "In as much as things seem to change, they always manage to remain the same." Whether it's in another country or on some foreign continent, it's always the same battle here at home. Can anyone tell me why?

"A NATION DIVIDED AGAINST ITSELF."

Together we stand. Yes, but divided we fall. That's the way I think we're headed.

Somehow we as a nation can stand, but not on the principals of individualism. We must get of the fanatics trend of I can do it alone.

"Every kingdom divided against it self is brought to desolation; and every city or house divided against it self shall not stand" (Matt.12–25, King James Version). It seems like we are at a place with so many forms of divisions, Democrats, Republicans, divided by two. Well that's okay, but what happened to the one nation? Because when one or the other parties is in control, only the same least three classes of peoples feel the pressures of denial. But it's all talk about the individual parties. There are conservative and liberals, divided by four, management and labor, divided by six white collar and blue collar, divided by eight, and we still have the north and south, divided not only by geographic standards either. There is super rich and the rich, divided by twelve, and the middle class, and the lower class, divided by fourteen the poor, not even in the equation. Now we haven't even looked at the demographic list yet.

Every such group thinks only within the boundaries of itself. We try so very hard to achieve that static of being individualistic somehow we have not yet figured out how, but trust me we're trying.

Webster says individualism is "the theory that individual freedom is as important as the welfare of the community or group as a whole (2) any ethical economic or political theory that emphasizes the importance of individuals. (3) Each for himself; absence of cooperation; wanting a separate existence for oneself." I agree with having our individual freedoms of speech, choice, etc. We've been told to become totally exiled and separated from each other. We have somehow lost the ability to think laterally;

society has found a way to have us for the most part narrow the point of our focus to one specific thing. This enables one to see the whole picture. This illusion of freedom I keep mentioning doesn't mean it's not available, I mean we have been given a reason not to exercise it. Different Agency Company or another official group, now that word "official" seems like it was made just to scare the pants off of the whole human family, to make sure we do exactly what we are told, without thinking. It works every time, and the illusion is, they make it seem so right, when they put in the political correctness system that was something like "pouring water over our heads and telling us it's raining."

With the politics today, I ask, who needs their correctness? And if we rely on the edict of today's political mannerism to proclaim our correctness, then we are in far worse condition than I thought.

Dwight D. Eisenhower was elected president, and John Fitzgerald Kennedy was elected senator of Massachusetts. The biggest news was Mr. Kennedy being the youngest senator ever elected to the United States Senate. The country was going through what I call a restoration period; we were at the end of two wars: from 1939 till 1945, WWII, then 1950 till 1953, Korea. Now trying to rebuild torn countries but never rebuilding torn societies, the people of each of these countries seems like they are always forgotten.

At the age of about fourteen, I was able to see where this nation was destined to go. I guess the evidence was very clear about this freedom; I really understand the real value of living free.

Looking back from the sixty-fifth milepost to the twelfth of my life, I am sure now more than ever the only thing is, it's not the separation of races only, but with various conditions means we're separated by different kinds of fears.

I have neither the resources nor the experience to do research, but my guess would be there are more doctors in every area, more millionaires in every area, and still there are more problems in every area. So the lack of either is not the solution to most of our problems, but we are still chasing that same illusion.

We as a nation have become so consumed with our own self- centeredness, and it looks like eventually we will become our own captors.

1976 was our nation's bicentennial, and some research revealed every nation that previously had risen to a respectable degree of power such as this one, after the two hundredth year the evidence of collapse and destruction became quite clear. All of them were defeated internally, and the major contributor was greed. It looks like we are headed down that same path to destruction.

The North American Indians learned the best way to catch the gray wolf. They sharpen a knife as sharp as possible, and then soak the knives with fresh animal blood. Then they pack snow tightly on the knife, soak it again, over and over each time packing it with snow, and then they place the knife in the ground, with the point protruding about an inch or so above the frozen ground. Then they pour fresh blood on the ground all around it. When the wolves get the scent of the fresh blood with, their keen sense of smell leads them right to it. Oh when they find it, then the licking begins. They lick the blood from the frozen snow and as they lick, the frigid snow deaden the tongue nerves, so they would not be able to feel the point of knife. The more they lick the closer they are to the point of no return. Their tongues has became so insensitive from the frozen snow, they continue licking, cutting their tongue. Yet because of the taste of fresh blood and their carnivorous nature, they don't know they were feasting on their own blood, so their demise is very near, and the next morning the trapper returns to find the dead wolf which has eaten himself to their death.

Now this wasn't meant to be something to laugh about. It's meant to show how some selfish motivated habits can come to not so good of an ending, and I do hope we realize where we are before it's to late.

Every past holds some pleasant and not so pleasant memories, but for the sake of rebuilding a better future, it would be good for all of us to take a look back and find a better way for moving forward. We see money doesn't do it, or all these things we bring into our lives, and we always return back to square one—lost. And the only thing that will ever work is love.

When I turned sixteen, with my parents' signature I joined the Illinois National Guard, still working at the grocery store, now as a stock/boy, but still making the same home delivers. These are some times I will never forget.

I think here is where all of what I had been taught back on the farm really started to make sense. Daddy always said, "listen, and then wait, and the time would come to use what you've heard and learned."

This new mix of a people was like the mix of all things that I had first learned about, even before I knew about this vast racial diversity. All I was able to see was people. But I did recognize they all had the same struggles of not knowing how to live free. But somehow we as a free nation still were not living free, yet the picture of freedom was more evident than before, especially for my family. The store changed owners three times while I was there, and I had become a part of the transaction. Each time the store changed owners, I was figured in the deal, and each time I received another five-dollar raise.

After a year or so at the store, the neighborhood started to become more integrated, and this was new. At first it was a very good merger, and I got another lifetime friend, Shaffer Ashman. His parents lived only four houses from the store. When they moved in the neighborhood, he was living in Florida with his farther and step-mom until he finished school. After that he moved to Chicago. Every Wednesday night was drill night I was assigned to company (H) 178th regimental combat team infantry heavy weapons. I must have weighed about 118 pounds at the time, but it was much excitement for all of us young boys. Plus it helped keep so many of us young boys out of trouble. My plan had always been to become a military man, and I was on my way. Our company commander was Captain Lester, E. Division; he was a father figure to us. We learned how to become soldiers, but more than that, we learned how to become better citizens in the process. His philosophy was basically that of my parents, only from a militarily standpoint. I must say he taught from two manuals, the military's and his own, and most of it was naturally his own. Then I met another longtime friend, Everett Redwell. He, Richard and I were good buddies, but Richard and I were good friends until later on. It was so strange that Everett, Richard, and Shaffer never were close, but I had three of the best friends anyone could ever have. Well the past life started to overtake me; that life I thought was over. Our armory was a very old building with the ceiling leaking, and our Caucasian fellow soldiers had a very new and modern building. Their equipment was quite new, and ours was very old, but we did well with what we had.

After the last family took over the store, they had enough help within their own family and they didn't need me anymore. I then started working at the (CBA) Chicago Bar Association where Laura and Fred was, located at 29 So. LaSalle Street. My greatest excitement was I was working with my brother and sister.

The $1.33 cents an hour never crossed my mind, and like all of the rest, I started washing pots and pans. Washing dishes was quite a job. One evening Mrs. Mae Johnson, who was the superintendent, asked me to come with her. She took me downstairs on the eleventh floor and told the hostess, "This is your buss boy; take care of him." This was really a step up for me. Later the waitresses asked, "Who do you know around here?" And I said, "Laura and Fred." She said, "Miss Johnson don't do something like this for anyone unless they are special." I told her maybe I was special. I didn't answer with a cocky attitude, just to say I really didn't know why she found favor in my performance.

And weeks later I was at my assigned work area, and here came Ms. Johnson again with that certain look on her face. She was a very attractive, professional and quite a pleasant lady, always a smile, she said, "Alton," "Yes maim," I said. "Hurry, go and comb your hair," she said. I did have hair in those days. "And tuck your shirt in very neatly and meet me in the main dining room, it's someone I want you to meet." I went to my locker and made myself look very neat. I went back down one flight of stairs and met her at the door. She said to just be myself, walking towards a table with one man seated reading a newspaper. When we approached the table where this gentleman was seated, "Alton," she said, "do you know whom this gentleman is?" "No ma'am," I replied. She said, "This is Senator John Kennedy from Massachusetts."

"Oh! How are you, sir?"

This man arose from his seat and extended his hand out to me and said, "It's a pleasure to meet you young man." Ms. Johnson said, "Mr. Kennedy is the youngest member of the United States Senate, Alton." And I said, "I remember seeing something about you on the news." "Yes it's been quite a bit," he said, and then he asked me how I liked working with people and working in a place like this, meaning always a lots of highly profile people I suppose. I said it's real good and then Ms. Johnson knew just when to end the conversation, then she very properly dismissed us by saying, "Alton is a very nice young boy," and this very distinguished young Senator said, "It's been a pleasure meeting you young man." I went back to doing my job. But I remember the kindness this man showed to a young boy whom he'd never seen before. Then came time to choosing a candidate for the Democratic Party, and guess who was chosen to represent his party? Yes, Mr. Kennedy. When he ran for president in the 1961 election, I said, "Oh, that's my friend." Working in a place like this gave me the opportunity to see the conduct of the rich and powerful. I was able to understand money and positions weren't the most important things in life, though neither is bad if it is handled properly. We all are just people, and all of us have our own struggles. It matters not what position one might be in.

At this time the political process was not that important to blacks. We had not yet earned that right, although we were a free people; or were we? But all other people were voting. There were people from Europe that couldn't speak English, but that was ok. As long as you weren't black (I think we were still called Negros at that time), you could vote.

Maybe the question might be asked, why not just do what

senator H. R. Clinton said, "It's time to put that part of history behind us and focus on the future"? Well if the system was meant to work for all people, then I ask, am I not one of those people? As long as nothing is said, nothing will ever get done. It's been said, "When all is said and done, but there's always more said than done."

I became intensely interested in learning about a multicural society that this nation has become. The elected officials started referring to the country as a melting pot, and it seemed as if they were trying to encourage some kind of disruption, because every time it was mentioned, it had a negative edge to it.

The evidence of gang activity became quite apparent all over the city. Gangs had names and each had their own signs, painted on every available wall on street signs, buildings, and sidewalks. But this lifestyle wasn't for me and besides, Daddy would probably made me wish I never heard of a gang. You could tell these young people never heard the word living free, and a great many (some I knew) lost their chance of ever being free by losing their lives to another falsehood. The adversary tells us this way is the best way; all you need is a little bit of this and a little bit of that. But he never tells what this or that really is.

I found ways to keep my mind occupied, with school and work. My job was second to school, and my friend Richard and I had established ourselves as the best track stars at Parker Elementary School. We got separated when we went to high-school because the district changed. I attended Englewood, and he went to Hyde-park, but we stayed friends and remained friends until now.

School and work were enough to keep me busy. On Friday there was always a dance at one of the schools. There were plenty dances for young people. Some schools and churches would open their recreation rooms to help the young people stay out of trouble.

Roller-skating was a very popular sport. When one of the singing stars was performing in town, some of them would always come by the rink to entertain and encourage us. They would always make it for the closing sessions. They would sing a couple of songs just to encourage all of us to stay in school, not get into trouble, and always obey our parents. Now that's a thing of the past. There are still some doing these things, but like then.

We were able to catch many of the most famous singers up close and personal. Diana Washington a local, Jerry Butler another local, and many others that wasn't local but always willing to stop by and give a song and say something encouraging, which was always needed. They knew we were caught up in the same place they once were, but in most cases today, the ones that are behind are trapped, and no one seems to care. I think real freedom will allow you to see where there's something wrong and try to fix it.

From 1837 to present, there have been forty-five mayors serving Chicago; forty-four men and one woman. I can't comment on the performance of only eight, and that would be just my opinion, which would not be fair to make that kind of judgment.

April 20, 1955Richard Joseph Daley was elected mayor of Chicago. He brought some brand-new ideas and a different approach of making things happen, and a new régime probably wasn't a bad idea.

However, judging from the time we arrived there in '52, not very much had been done since 1837. Now it was time for some changes, and Mr. Daly was ready to do so.

The Windy City was showing signs of physical neglect and

moral decay. Prostitution was legal; the state provided monthly check-ups for the ladies. Gambling was ok; that's before the state took control of it. The city was quite trashy to say the least. The Southern winds of racial tension and unrest were blowing strong. The civil rights movement was gaining a little momentum. This made the political leaders nervous about angering the white citizens for doing what they were supposed to have done. Promising things will soon get better something like now, this man had a real shot at becoming a dictator with a genuine plantation-style politics. He was able to make some good things happen, but as was always the case with a hidden agenda, somehow he was always able to pull it off. He spent the first part of the first term re-organizing the political structure by creating what was known as the Daley machine, by swapping jobs for votes. This was a no-brainier, especially for the black men, white women, and a few other minority citizens. This process helped speed up the time process for black Americans to have the chance to vote, which should already have been done. On December 1, 1955, Rosa Parks decided that was the day she was not going to give up her seat. Standing does some things and sitting does some, so she decided to remain seated, and look what happened.

That started the historic wheels rolling towards some distribution of justice. Her actions, or non-actions, and her subsequence arrest triggered a 381-day boycott of the buses by blacks. The city's black population helped spark the nation's civil rights movement. My question still is, in 1955, in these United States of free America, why was this allowed to continue? I still cannot understand why. There were countless brutal murders committed by that same old traditional, well-protected, hood-wearing group the KKK. During the civil rights struggle, we saw the murdering of Emmit Till. Fred Hampton and Bobby Clark, who were members of the Black Panther Party, were also murdered during this time. But Mr. Hoover, director of the F.B.I., said they were trying to overthrow the federal government. So they had to take whatever steps were necessary to stop them, and trust me, they did just that. Still again, these were the people who were elected to protect us, and they allowed this to happen. Even now in most places when the rights of a very few citizens are violated there's nothing done, but we all are a "Free People One Nation." Well something is still wrong. It was often said that Chicago had the best politicians that money could buy, and other parts of the nation as well.

The Chicago Police Department was so corrupted, any and everything was going on right in the open, and with his national political strength, Mr. Daly brought plenty federal funded programs to a very parched city.

One of the first undertakings in the early Sixties was when Mr. Daily was to reform the police department. He appointed a 15-member committee to make a plan to achieve this process. They recommended that an outsider be brought in to head-up the police department, and that person was Orlando Winfield Wilson. Before becoming superintendent of police in Chicago, Mr. Wilson was very well known to the law enforcement communities. He continued the movement toward the professionalization of the police begun by August Vollmer, A protégé of Vollmer, Wilson studied under Vollmer at the University at Berkeley and worked for Vollmer as a Berkeley police officer. Wilson eventually became chief of police at Fullerton, California; Wichita, Kansas; and superintendent of the Chicago police. One of Mr. Wilson's great strengths was his firm belief in honest law enforcement. He became known as the reform chief. This reputation earned him an invitation to bring professional police management to the Chicago police.

His idea was that corruption was the byproduct of poor organization, bad planning, and bad lines of command. The outcry was heard all over about an outsider coming in to change our law enforcement system. Mayor Daily said all available people were already corrupt, so he wanted someone with no ties to the city. Mr. Wilson was the man. He knew that the police had very little control over the root cause of crime, but he developed the concept of preventive patrol. He believed an aggressive police force could stiffen criminal behavior by the reduction of the opportunity for crime like his protégé Vollmer. Like always, the more you see change, the more you see things remain the same.

In April 1957, Everett and I enlisted in a six month advanced combat readiness training program that was offered by the (USNG) United States National Guard that was supposed to "help with our education." Wrong. When we arrived at ft. Leanordwood Mo, then we knew what was going on. It was a special training mission for Vietnam, and there was nothing said about education, but we had to make the best out of that situation, and situation it was.

I had thought most of my life about making a full career in the military, but after being there right away, the same ole song started playing over again. The racial injustice was just as harsh for Blacks, Mexicans, Jews, and Puerto Ricans as it was in Georgia. What was so spirit damaging was that we were being trained to go thousands of miles somewhere we had never heard of to fight, and we had a daily battle right in our barracks. When we went on leave, the eating arrangements were just like in Georgia. We were going to free a people in Laos, Vietnam, and our situation was still the same; and in most cases it still hasn't changed yet. After work was over, we would go to the movie. Every time, there would be a fight between these races of soldiers in the United States Army. Reverend Martin Luther King, Jr. had clouds of dust on the rise. The backlash didn't ease our situation at all, unless we had a sergeant of color around, and that was just as scarce as hen teeth. All of the extra duties, and we of course would get the last part of the bull that goes over the fence. There was a Jewish soldier in my platoon who was smarter than anyone else. They gave him every meager and demeaning job they could find, and with a very pugnacious attitude towards him every time they would approach him. It was just horrible to see from an audience point of view. I was used to having this kind of treatment done to me, but this was the first time I was on the viewing end, and it looked even worse. Maybe I thought I was more capable of handling it, seeing I had many years of practice, but he handled it with a laugh. They said there were already to many Jews in height places in this country, and they just laughed about it.

There were so many times they tried to break this young man, but we all kept him protected as much as we could. This young man went through absolute torture; he would do different things for people just to have someplace to hide. They would do things pretending it was just out of fun, but there was no fun in that at all. In my platoon, there were only three blacks in basic training, but we were busy learning about what we were there for. After the first eight weeks, we were given a fifteen-day leave. After leave, I went to Ft. Jackson, South Carolina, for advanced training. This is where I really understood what racism was. The difference in where I was then and where I was born and spent the first twelve years of my life, I didn't have any contact with the whites. As long as they say jump and we jumped then there was no reason to change, but now we were suppose to be on a equal and more level playing field so the M.L.R. (meaning the main line of résistance) automatically kicked in, and this became very serious. So Everett and I gathered all of the blacks from throughout the battalion so we would be able to survive. I must remind you this wasn't in South Vietnam or the Ivory Coast of Africa; this happened right on the soils of America. You know, the land of the free. Now the first thing came to my mind was, how were my uncle and his black fellow comrades treated in the earlier war? Then and even more now, this thing call freedom is just an illusion. After we got settled in at this new fort, we had more liberties. Every Friday when we finished, we were good to go unless it was my guard duty.

One Friday, several of us—I was the only non-white in the bunch this particular time—received a non-restrictive three-day pass, meaning you could go anywhere you wanted as long as you were back for check in Monday morning. Many would go home if they could afford it. This time we just went to town, and this town was Columbia, South Carolina. We went to the Greyhound bus station where there was a restaurant, cafeteria style. We got out trays and made our selection. We went to pay and every one paid except me. When I started to pay I was told "We can't serve you here you will have to leave." And a friend from Chicago his name was Greer, an Italian, and another's his name was John H., which I did not know either before fort Jackson, said, "What the blank you mean?" She replied, "That's the law, I have to do what I'm told, please don't make trouble for me please." Greer said,

"Where do he suppose to get his food?" She said, "Around the corner in the back of the building." They required their money back and someone said let's see what she mean. We went back to my dining area, and it looked like where we would slop the hogs back in Georgia on the farm. What bothered me about that situation was I was in a military uniform, being trained to go somewhere to give my life to protect this freedom here at home. Freedom; is it real? Or is it just an illusion? I still say the latter.

We returned to post the same night and finished our week-end pass on post. Monday we reported it to the sergeant, and that was the end of that. The c/o company commander said it was out of jurisdiction, and nothing could be done about it, He told me to just not go back again, and that was the end to that story.

After awhile we were put on a three-week alert, waiting to go away to some far distant land to kill someone we never knew. I wondered if this was another way of just taking some of us blacks somewhere to leave us in some wooded field, like so many had been left in Georgia. There were different things we thought about. But a marine division went to Laos where the Vietnam warfare began, and shortly after they arrived, it was over. We were no longer on that alert, and that didn't make any-one unhappy. We spent lots of evenings at the gym, where one of my basketball friends was John Havelochezk; he really was a fun and a very kind person.

After the crises were over, we got orders to go to different forts. I was sent to Fort Riley, Kansas. Well, this for me was just fine. I had already decided that a military career wasn't what I wanted. But this move was o.k. I had been promoted to spec.3rd class, and they needed advanced solders to train incoming troops. That's what I did until I left on October, 6, 1957, when I returned home.

There is always something very special about coming home. Maybe you have been on a vacation and had a great time, but when it's time to come home, it's even more special. I was only away for just a few days past six months, but it seemed like much longer than that. Fred had gotten my first driving license when I returned, and I thought that was a great thing one could do for another. I certainly realized that nothing had changed and probably never would, but I was now sure of my place in this society.

I imagined somewhere along the way I must have grown beyond the thought of having a fair chance at ever becoming free under the regular rim of the understanding of freedom, but what I did have and still have is ability to live a free life, in the midst of a society of people that think they are free and still living a life of constant confinement which is controlled by their fears. And I mean theirs because it's ones choice.

I started to pay attention to this political system during the Eisenhower Administration, and since then I have seen many changes in the two parties. There has never been a continuing progress of things that benefit the general public. I often wondered why, when one party or the other is in the controlling seat, whether it's the president or the senate or congress, the minority parties' members still live the same luxury life style. And the rest of the population it matters not what their political party may be. Their situation always remains the same or worse. One thing Daddy told us from the time he went to Sears and applied for credit, he qualified for a $1,500 credit limit, and this was a big piece of dough at that time, and they told him if you keep your credit in good standing you can get anything you need, well that was passed down to all of us. And this I see is just a system that the entire population now has become in slaved to. I think in the next fifty years, everybody will be totally debt controlled, and along with that we will be prisoners on the outside of the lockup stations. Free speech will be a thing of the past, freedom of independent movement will be limited, the right to any form of privacy will no longer exist, which that's already very much the norm today. The right to vote will not be needed. All of these things will be of the past. As we have seen in the last two presidential elections, the individual vote had absolutely nothing to do with the outcome. When we become felons by design rather than by committing a crime, as we were in the great South, that's when the real controlling takes place. Now a felon by committing a crime, voting is one of the rights they lose other than the right of independent movement. The credit system will soon change, and the majority of tax payers will be in an economic penitentiary, thus losing their right to participate in any elections process. See voting isn't a right, it's a privilege, as is the privilege to drive a automobile, because privilege's, can and soon will be taken away.

Penitentiary, according to Webster, is "a place for imprisonment, reformatory discipline or punishment, in the US, a state or federal institution for serious offenders. "Offenders" means "a violation or breaking of a social or moral rule; transgression; sin." According to the Holy Bible which I believe completely, outstanding and ongoing debt is a sin. How much do we hear about the individual debt and what a serious problem the American consumer has? Like these federal and local power thirsty agencies are always advertising, as if they themselves are not one of the consumer.

There are people today who are owned by the credit card industry, which I believe is illegally charging these enormous amounts of interests. But the federal regulations bureau says it's ok, but what would you expect? They are all of the same. We have been given another sleeping pill about this freedom system we're in. When we lose the ability to think for ourselves, we better know who's doing the thinking for us. I don't think this governmental system we have is thinking the best things for the people. We have given our lives over to the powers of self-possessions. We are taught excellence over morality, prosperity over humility, achieving over thoughtfulness, acquiring over sharing, and possession over all.

Today's independent or capitol and individual wealth is greater today than ever before, but so is the moral decay. All areas of crime are at their highest. The level of violence, drugs, child and spousal abuse, home invasions, and homicide is as if the assailant has the right to just kill the victim at will, just because. Community and family interaction has declined at a record-breaking rate. Friendly relationships are hardly mentioned. Education throughout the nation is nothing shorter than poor. Homelessness is steadily on the rise. More young people and women are joining this horrible statistic, but we are so into the just me, myself and I pattern, until none of this makes any difference to us. But that's just what we are taught. The best way to overcome a giant is to learn where his strength lies, and the strength of this giant isn't in its wealth. It's his numbers, and those numbers are the people. The method of divide and conquer is a system that's been in place for a long time, and it's working just fine.

Daddy told me to come to the plant where he was working and make out an application. I did and started working the next week. Here again, this was a big deal for me. Having the opportunity to work with my daddy and brother was quite a contrast from working together on the farm. I was much older and somewhat wiser. This step was a real cut above average for me.

I started with wages about six dollars and twenty-five cents an hour. This was good for me and the family, because I could be of more help for Daddy and support for the house. Remember, Sears had extended Daddy's credit. He was hooked. That word "credit" is just where the banks and insurance company want us, and most of us will never get free of it.

The only legacy a great deal of the population has is the idea that a good credit rating is all you need. That's what we were taught, and every year the national consumer debt gets higher and higher. I would guess today, more people are in a situational debt condition they will never be able to pay off.

Not because they can't, as much as they don't know how. It's not in our society's norm to live debt free, because we were never taught how. We were taught the only way is good credit.

I worked there until late 1959; Daddy and Fred lasted until the plant closed in 1960. The summer of 1958, I met a very special person. One Sunday afternoon after a baseball game at Washington Park, I was sitting with my family, just relaxing. Our doorbell rang. I answered the door, and a longtime friend and his wife and another beautiful young were there. We went upstairs; we lived on the second floor. Marcello and his wife, Jo-Ann Henderson, proceeded to make introductions. "Mr. And Mrs. Harvey this is my cousin from West Virginia, Mary Lee, and Bowie don't tell anybody but this is my nickname, Mary Lee Coles. We are going out for awhile and I thought you might want to join us." "Thank you but I must decline, I hasn't clean up from playing ball, and I have to be at work very early in the morning maybe another time," I said and Marty said, "Oh she will be here for a week or so." "Oh, good," I said. "I hope to see you again soon." "Maybe," she replied.

And they left and that next day. I couldn't get her off my mind. I saw her on one other occasion and asked if I could call her sometime. She said, "I think that would be ok." After a few days, I saw Marty again. What inspired me to tell him I was going to marry his cousin, I don't know, but that's what I said.

Looking back forty-four years later, I realize I am very glad I made that statement. The joys we've shared have been far greater than the pains of overcoming the trials that come with life. I must say it wasn't without some pain that was caused by our individual shortcomings, but we always had the love for each other and the respect for each other as individuals. She was in her junior year in high school. She returned home to complete school. I bought a car the next year and drove to West Virginia to see her, and I met her mother, Ms. Emma Coles. We only stayed over the weekend, but as we drove, I just knew this young lady would soon be my wife. So we returned home, and it seemed like somehow the evidence of things really changing was starting to show.

The job market made a complete shift, but the new plantation owner, Mayor Richard Daley, was preparing his next implementation of his new style of reformation of city government, by what became the Daley machine. He did this by cashing in on a resource that had been long ignored, which was the black vote. What he did was organize the ward system. The first thing was to teach blacks how to vote. This was a long process because voting was a very new concept for all blacks. There was some fear with this. See this was a very crucial and new experience for these new voters, because a great deal of them was new immigrants from different parts of the South where voting was just short of a complete thought. The memories of what kept them from voting back there.

Yes, there was some hesitation involved, but Mr. Daley was determining to accomplish his visionary plan. One of the plans was addition by dividing. He first divided the city into wards; then he added different job titles, making jobs for more black people that they never knew could be possible. Then he saw another wasted opportunity within the forgotten Hispanic community. Oh, there were some blacks who had been mentally enslaved to the thinking they were better than those who just left the fields. Just a repeat from the way it was back on the farm. I try very hard to refrain from this title, but it was the house niggers not associating with the field niggers. Then one was over the field (ones) and the house (ones) was taught they were better then the field (ones) and the head (one) was told he was better than the (ones) who was doing the work, but never equal to the whites, "you know" just like now.

While police superintendent Orlando W. Wilson was making some positive changes within the ranks police department, he still had some very difficult challenges, but for the most part he dealt with it.

Mr. Daley began a complete renovation of the south side of the city, which brought on a great deal of controversy. He bought all of the homes from the blacks and built seventeen story hi-rise buildings, which were nothing more than concentration camps. But remember, all of the black leaders were already handcuffed to that Daley machine called their jobs. So peoples lost homes to a take-it-or-leave it program, but he had enough political influence where he did whatever he wanted.

As the momentum of the civil rights movement increased, so did the backlash of violence. The same people we had known for so many years suddenly vanished into the ranks of denial and the evidence of the fallen tree, "when nobody's around does it make a sound?" I say yes, just as loud as if the arena is filled to capacity. "Everything remains invisible until it's looked upon."

My conversations to West Virginia had increased by far, and things looked really good for me. I had asked her, meaning Mary, what her plans were after she finished school. At this point, the only thing she knew was it was not going to be there.

Then I started to put plan B into action. I said, "Why not just stop through Chicago and live with Marty and Jo-Anne until you decided what you really wanted to do?" Well, that sounded ok for her at the time.

But more and more those visits from the past kept appearing. When I would go looking for work, I would get turned down for no reason other than color. Then along came some good old boys that would have jobs for sale, and again when the whites bought jobs they had them for life. But when we bought them after a couple of weeks of work we would be laid off, so the broken record continued playing.

Well here it comes again, Daddy had somehow saved enough money for a down payment on a house, five hundred dollars worth. The price was fourteen thousand and nine hundred dollars, but the bad thing was, very few black people could get a mortgage. They all had to buy a house on a contract, and it was always some hidden clauses where they couldn't understand. And when the realtor got ready they just forced them out, everything lost. Well, this was another one of those "same soup deals just warmed over" like back in Georgia. You know, anything goes; not much different now. My family has always been involved in belonging in and supporting the local church. The Baptist denomination is where we practice our faith, at this time we worshiped at the greater Mount Hope Baptist Church, pastored by Rev. William Lambert. This is the pastor that married my wife and me. His family was about the same size as ours. We grew very close over the years. Daddy served as one of the deacons. Gee and I sang in the choir, and later I was serving as a junior deacon along with my farther.

After doing anything I could to make an honest day's pay, another hometown fellow, George Emery, we hadn't seen since we left Georgia, was working for Mr. Hugh Hefner at the resident 1340 N, State Park Way. They needed people to do general housekeeping. Now this was a real shocker for this young back woodsy trying to become a big city sophisticated Christian raised country boy. It was a very interesting experience, and it wasn't just having breakfast with Mr. Playboy himself. Every morning when he was in town, there were plenty very beautiful people there other than Mr. H.

He often shared his stories of the struggles that came before the young business took root. It seemed like a huge explosion, and as the story goes, "and the rest is history." This is one of the times "history" is personified because it was "his story. I am glad I had the awesome opportunity to have the story told to me by the one who lived it. After a few days on the job and accepting the horror of reality that the world I was now a small part of, would never be a part of anything of my future than it was just a job. But still very beautiful Mr. H. had probably all of his old shirts very neatly hanging in his closet near the backside, the collars was worn and once I asked him why he kept them. He said those were the things he once had to wear, and he wanted to remember the times when those were all he had. He said he'd like to go back in his thoughts so he could always remember where he had come from.

Mary graduated in June of '61, and as I had hoped, she did come back to Chicago. So far, my plans were working well. I took her job searching. She was above average in typing, but every place we went was not hiring a typist; but what they weren't hiring was black typist. See, the great wheels of justice were rolling, but as always in the opposite direction. But we never stopped trying. Not so long and after a few rejections, she got a job at Zenith, working on the assembly line this wasn't to good for women. See, chivalry wasn't gone yet, but she stayed there for awhile.

I was still not working on a steady job, but I was painting much of the time, which was a trade I'd learned back home in the 4H club. This was one of the most popular and positive programs that was available for all young people then. What I learned became a great benefit.

The race was now on for the presidential election coming up in November of 1961. The candidates were: Richard M. Nixon (Republican), and my old friend Senator John Fitzgerald Kennedy (Democrat), whom I met a few years earlier.

While everybody was trying to adjust to the every Tuesday morning air-raid sounds at 10:30 a.m., The United States and the Soviet Union were flexing their muscles about their nuclear powers. The biggest talk from this side of the Atlantic was the intercontinental ballistic missiles, but the war of our fear was greater than the fears of war. It had been about fourteen years since the Cold War had hit the scene, and the thing that this country went to Europe to stop. Those were then their greatest fears; while of course the United States had won the war and there were jobs, money, and yes freedom, the country felt threatened of the spread of communism. I am still wrestling with this thing we know as freedom. The fields of the post war gave birth to a new generation of conformity and counterculture. When the entire middle class of America picked up and abandoned the inner cities and headed to the suburbs, millions of middle class Americans settled into their own zones of comfortable lives. They left generations of torn-down buildings and rat-infested and depressing ghettos for the financial dysfunctions to inherit. But the services that was there, well, they went as well.

The civil rights movement was gaining momentum along with the beat of the rock and roll bands and the feminism movement.

The recovery of the economy of the postwar and the contribution to a prosperous life came through the GI Bill. It was a difficult period between President Truman and President Eisenhower. They were faced with coming out of a bitter World War II and fighting what seemed like a losing Cold War battle with China and the Soviet Union. What I wasn't aware of was that this was nothing new. It had been going on a long time before, but we could not see or hear of it. It made it seem like this was a brand new world, but as we said, "Everything remains invisible until it's discovered."

The relationship between Mary and I became quit strong. I told her from the very beginning that I was looking for a wife, and I didn't want to waste her time or mine. So we agreed to just keep seeing each other and see where it was going to go. Well, I can tell you that all was going well in my favor. Rosie Lee was married and divorced and back in Chicago with her four children, Kenneth, Melvin, Marietta, and Arthur Jr. Laura and Fred got married in 1957 while I was away for military training.

Now it's time for me to go for the gold, and did I strike

it rich? October 28, 1961, we were joined in holy matrimony. We were married in my parents' home. I think other than the fact I was marrying the girl I loved beyond description, getting married right at home was the best. I was still working at the penthouse; still making twenty-five dollars a day, and I could see there was a need for me to start seeking something better. I was still painting and doing whatever I could to make things better. Mary and I often visit our past and just thank God for how he's kept us. We had gone to a jewelry store and put her rings on a layaway plan. One hundred and twenty-five dollars and when the time came I couldn't' get them out. Mother came to the rescuer. I told Mom, and Mom smiled and said to ask my future wife if she would mind getting marred using her rings. Now Mary was Daddy's very special friend, and Mom loved her also. I asked her if she would mind wearing my mom's rings, and to my surprise she said she would be honored. So that's the way we began our journey, and it has been nothing shorter than blessed and beautiful. Laura Ann didn't like the idea that much because she and I were the perfect boy and girl first cousins. Laura Ann and I had been running buddies from the time we moved from Michigan, and she couldn't imagine us not running the streets any more together. We used to go dancing. We would enter dance contests and always win, but we knew every road had to end somewhere. While really loving Mary, but still losing her running buddy, all is well with them today. There is another aunt who was very close to me. She was Uncle Ulysses (Buddy), Dad's youngest brother's wife. Her name was Freda. They were my favorite couple. I thought their marriage was another good model for me to focus on. Freda would always encourage me and tell me not to ever let anything keep me from doing whatever I wanted to do.

She never had to add as long as it's right. As Daddy would say, if you fail, always fail trying. We kind of grew up tougher. They had one daughter, Seder, and I did lots of babysitting for them. I basically stayed with them during the summer months for many years. He's gone now, and she lives in California. We are still the best of friends. I talk with her quit frequently, and we have many precious memories to share. I thank God that she was always there for me. Now we're closing the doors on our young lives, but as we've learned, God will always open new ones.

Mayor Daley launched a Hugh Freeway construction project, and that brought more jobs for minorities; and yes, I qualified. I worked there for one contractor, but after he finished, he sent me to another one and I started with him. The first thing I did was give my wife her own rings. What bothered me the most was no matter where I went and whatever was going on, it always had the same flavor of racism. It was no different from Georgia except they just changed the color of their hoods and sheets to two- and three- piece suits.

President John F. Kennedy was trying to put together what is known as a comprehensive plan for the nation. He spoke about embarking upon a new frontier, but he was dealing with the growing tension of what some thought was leading to an inevitable all-out racial war between whites and blacks. The anger that was brought on from the brutal lynching of a 14-year-old boy, Emmett Louis Till, that took place in Money Mississippi, August 28, 1955. This was an event that struck the black communities with a staggering blow.

These are some of the things that have been going on from the time our people got on that first ship that arrived from Africa.

I am still asking why. The sounds of the sonic booms were

heard all through the day, every day. This is when they were breaking the sound barrier by flying these jet planes faster than the speed of sound. With all of the other stuff going on around, it made it somewhat difficult to keep focused on any objective. Again, it's always easier to return back to what you know. I did wonder if it would have been better if daddy had stayed in Georgia, but I'm glad he was the one to make those decisions, because he knew what was best for his family.

All the wars we've participated in seem like something would of changed other than we the people now have the opportunity to bear all of the expenses, and lose a few more inches of that freedom. And in a short time we all see just what I've been talking about, that freedom isn't, but the illusion is real.

My choice of sport now changed along with other changes that come with growing up. I found a great interest in the sport of bowling, which I still do. I became quite good, and after a couple of years, I had reached a average of about 185. I thought very strongly about joining the professional tours, but I bet you can't guess. Well, I was born black, and blacks couldn't join the tour. You know, having full rights under the law, so I as many others just bowled in leagues and played in some local tournaments. There was a city single and double tournament held at the Miami Bowling Alley (in Chicago). A friend named Charlie Hunter and I entered in the doubles set. They had plain-clothes police guarding because the two of us were bowling in the tournament, but it was for our safety. This was not in Georgia, neither was it in South Africa, but it was in Chicago, Illinois, around 1962. What part of this freedom belonged to me then and now?

My wife announced that we were going to be parents; what? You're not kidding me, are you? Well, no. This was the greatest news I could have heard. But during the pre-natal care on our first visit, there were x-rays taken. But before our next visit, we were notified to make a unscheduled visit and informed that my wife had tuberculosis. Well, this was to say the least a major piece of news we didn't want to hear, but we used a method that we had learned and used plenty of times before—prayer. Our doctor, Dr. John H. Meyer, a very good man he told us don't worry every thing would be just fine. But my wife would have to take a shot twice a week until her time to deliver, so with much prayer and taking the doctor's advice, everything went well. About a week before her time came to deliver, we had to travel about twenty miles to a state tuberculosis institution (MTS). This was very difficult for me, having to travel on public transportation, but I was there every day, not reluctantly but more joyously. I was alloyed to stay until about ten o'clock, but I would leave around nine to make good connections with the buses.

On March 27, early in the morning, I got a call from the hospital that she was in labor. I hurried to get there. I arrived about nine a.m., and the baby was born at 1:07 p.m. They let me stay with her through the entire birth. No, I didn't pass out. Our first child of three had arrived. It was a boy, Alton Jr. He was four pounds and eleven ounces. He had to stay until he reached at least five pounds, and she had to stay about a month after his birth to make sure she was cured, and she was.

The young baby gained the necessary weight in about two or three weeks, and I brought him home. We were living with my parents. We lived on the second floor. My mother and sisters were there to assist me, but for the most part this was just a repeat. I had three younger sisters, so I had practice with diaper duties. Mom and the others were willing to help. I could hardly wait to go to the hospital every day, and when the time came for her to come home, I couldn't keep my cool. Tears of joy were flowing from all of us.

Mom had everything ready when she arrived. She had not seen him for about three weeks, so this was a very happy time for everybody. By the time she came home, between Daddy and me, we had this baby pretty well spoiled, so she said. After looking seem like for ever for work, I asked Daddy what he thought about me trying this politics game. Now we were voting and it wasn't one of his best subjects. His theory was you would have to wear too many different faces, none of which was honest. I now wonder how he knew that. I was working at one of the small chain supermarkets, Veto's, a family name Veto (Marsha pinto). I was also serving as an assistant present captain, one who would make sure every eligible voter was registered. In exchange, you would get a city job. I had worked at Veto's for about a year. I was hired at one of the county hospitals where convalescent patients were treated, which was a pretty gruesome and a painful place to work. But I learned quite a lot of humility and thankfulness of what we had rather than what we didn't have. It seems like there's a lesson around every corner, waiting to be learned if we just prepare ourselves to learn.

This wasn't the worst place to work, but transportation wasn't the best, and the pay was even worse. But I hung in there until something better came along.

At this time, with the situation with the Soviet Union and Southeast Asia and the civil rights movement here in America, everything was very unstable.

I've watched from the 34 president to the 43. I can't see anything that was done from President Eisenhower's administration up to the present time that has done anything that has lasted anytime. Seems to me every time we elect another president, he starts promising the same things the last one promised, and nothing ever gets completed. The education in the entire country is worse than horrible. They've been talking about balancing the budget for time un-end. Every newly elected president first starts spending in every direction except here.

The only thing that has endured is taxes. We are paying more and getting less. Our health and medical situation is just about at the point of collapse. You would think these people we keep re-electing to manage the business would know what they're doing by now, but they keep telling us things are getting better, and for the most part, most of us really believe it; just as they believe they're really free. Mom left for Pittsburgh early in the summer of 1962. She went around the middle of June to visit her uncles, who were her mother's brothers. Dad would make sure she had a vacation. She was gone about a month, but this time things were somewhat different. Mom was supposed to have stayed for a month, but she called and said she was ready to come home, which was just what we wanted to hear. She was supposed to arrive by train on July 10, but she called and said her train was delayed and she would arrive at 8:30 Monday the 12. Sunday night the 11, around 10:30, Daddy had a stroke. I remember Laura came upstairs and told me to come down; something was wrong with Daddy. Mary and I went down and found Daddy sitting on the side of his bed. I said to him, "You feel like boxing, young fellow?" just trying to cheer him up, like we always had done in the past. He looked at me and said, "Son, Daddy's tired and my fighting is over." I knew that wasn't what I wanted to hear. This is the last thing he said to me. The 911 call was made, and he was taken to the hospital.

This was definitely a very hard thing for us. When we met Mom at the train station, she could just tell something wasn't right. The first thing she asked was, "Where's Douglas?" We told her he was in the hospital. We didn't know about daddy's death until after nine o'clock, when I called the hospital. They told us he had expired at 8:30 that morning. Mom called everybody together and told us to pray. I led us in prayer as I had many times before. Then Mom said that it was my father's and her agreement that if he was the first one to go, Bowie, meaning me, would be the one to make the final decisions for this family. And every body was ok with that, so that's the way we kept things right up until now. This meant Daddy wasn't around anymore, and this was very devastating to say the least. This was an experience we hadn't had since Mama Ethel, but what we had been taught was now ready for display. Now Momma and me had to make all of the decisions for the household, and with the support of the rest of the gang, everything worked just fine.

It seemed like everything I had been taught all came back, like when you study for an exam. You're nervous at the beginning, but soon the information that was stored just starts to flow. How glad I was when Daddy told us years ago, "When I tell you something, I want you to listen." I see the learning isn't in understanding; it's in the listening, and I have learned to listen more than I speak. But most of the people I know will not agree with this statement.

The Cuban missile crisis occurred in October 1962, when the United States learned that the Soviet Union had secretly installed missiles in Cuba, which is only about 90 miles from

Florida. These bad fellows were ready to launch a nuclear attack, probably on any America city. I remember leaving my wife and our newly born son home with my mother and five sisters. I was going to work. My starting time was eight o'clock. I told Mary I loved her. I was truly thinking I would never see them again, at least on this side of heaven. This was a day I will never forget, and I'm sure many won't, either. The Cuban Missile Crisis had played to the final end. President Kennedy had given Nikita Khrushchev a final ultimatum for the removal of the Soviet war ships, from where I suppose they were to close to national waters. But he was given a direct order and time they must return, which was 10:30 a.m. Tuesday morning. Mr. Kennedy said if you don't remove them, then I will blow them out, and the entire world was on edge. You talk about the day the earth stood sill; well, that was it. If my memory serves me true, at about 10:10, those ships were ordered by Mr. Khrushchev to turn back. It was reported "the clock of doom" stopped at 11:55 a.m. It was said if had it reached 12:00 noon, it would have been the full and final destruction of the human race.

The Soviet Union had placed the missiles in Cuba earlier in 1962, after the Cuban leaders believed the United States were going to attack the small island. Cuba was a friendly alley with the Soviet Union, but President Kennedy told Nikita he had to remove those missiles. The tension was rapidly building, and the whole world was afraid. The skies were busy with fighter jets all day, everyday. Some years ago, a movie called The Day the Earth Stood Still; this was a perfect example of that movie.

Times were very difficult during these years, but we were pretty much used to hard times coming from the background we did. Fear had always been a capable subject in the Harvey household, but this was the first time we had to face it without our father. But we always met fears with faith. Now I realize what it means when it says, "Your life continues long after you're gone." This I think is when I started to live my life through the teaching of my father. Mom was there to remind me what Daddy would have liked me to do. She wasn't telling me how to do a particular thing; what she was doing was reminding me how to use what had been given to me. Now both are gone, and I'm still using what they gave me.

Some may say, why all the complaining? That's ok, but the fact of the matter is I wouldn't have it any other way.

My parents were not intellectually tottered, but they were profoundly intelligent.

In our life travels, before we began to give ourselves great cheers, I think, there are so many people who became involved in my life, and I must tell something about the Spotsers. We met this family in 1962. We were new members at the Kendrick Memorial M-B Church, Pastured by Rev. AD Spriggs. The Spotsers, Jimmy Evelyn's and (3) children Layette Fulton and Enid. Jimmy was a fireman but more importantly, he was a man with integrity, a person with good moral values, you know a person that a community loved having around.

Our three children and theirs were about the same in ages. Our families became very good friends. Jimmy and I served on the deacon board of our church for many years until early in the Seventies. His health started to fail. He would make frequent visits to the doctor. Not long after these visits, Evelyn told me the tests that they had been doing concluded he had cancer. Well, now, this was a real shocker, but we had to deal with it. The point I'm trying to make is not how great I am, but how blessed I am.

One Sunday after service, Jimmy asked me if I was busy on the following Tuesday. Well, I said Tuesday was not a free day. I had some labor union business to attend to. I asked if I could be of help another day. He said Wednesday would be just fine. I said, ok, what's up? He said, "Oh, I want you to go fishing with me."

"Well, that's good," I said. "Then I'll pick you up about 6 :00 am." We went to Starveed-Rock about 100 miles southwest of Chicago, near a small town name Utica, Ill. It's a very popular state park area, but about half way there, he started to tell me some very personal business matters concerning his family. I started to talk about something else, and he told me not to worry about that, but for me to listen to what he were telling me. Well, that stopped me right in my tracks. Then I saw he wanted my attention. He said, "I want you to look after my family." Then I said, "Jimmy, you know I'll do whatever need doing. I'll help you." Again, he said, "Listen to me. I need you to take care of my family for me." I gave him my word. Then he said, "I'm going to Texas to see my granddaughter for Thanksgiving," which was about three weeks from our outing. That's where he went home to be with our Lord. Please don't take this lightly, because I can't imagine anything could be more humbling in my life, for a friend to choose me to oversee his family. He passed away Thanksgiving Day of 1979. Evelyn and the children and grandchildren are doing well.

My parents were intellectually untutored but profoundly intelligent, so what they were giving us was the lesson on how to be free citizens and how to live a free life. I kept trying to see what was really different from Georgia. Some twenty years later, there were places in Chicago where the signs read "members only." But those members probably were those good old boys.

I find myself trying to remember if our parents ever told us they expected or even wanted us to become successful. I don't think so. But we were expected to always love each other, and to, always stand for truth and righteousness. Now I understand; that's the real meaning of success. Now here comes the big one. What does the dictionary say about success? It says it is a favorable result, the gaining of wealth, and/or fame, etc. "Successful": turning out as was hoped for, having gained wealth, fame, etc. Well, you got me. But what would have happened if all of the farmers there was working year after year and never received one cent for their labors said one day, "We're not going to plant another grain." What would have happened to the food supply? Had we not been successful in continuing our planting, cultivating, and gathering, and hauling it to town where it could be dispatched all over the country, well I have a little different opinion with the meaning of the word success. I never gained the wealth; neither am I a famous person, but I have always progressed. I will always be in the line that reads "servant needed," and if I never become successful according to the standards of modern society, then I've used the teachings I received quite well.

After joining the regular democratic organization, learning the proper steps in the voter's registration process, and knocking on many doors trying to get people registered to vote, this was a real task. First helping people or telling people to do something they never did before, still there were places in the South still lynching for doing the same things. I was given a job at one of the hospitals ran by the county. I worked there for about a year, and I got a job with the Chicago park district as a park attendant—that's a janitor. I tried to get into the painters' union, but you would never guess why I didn't. You see, when I was born, somehow my color didn't match the color line the city was using. So I did what most of us have always done. I caught the crumbs that fell from the table of ole Massey, but the park district was much better.

I never did understand what the regular Democratic Party meant. I'm glad I didn't wind up with that ill-regular party, but it was a blessing for Mary and me especially after she told me it would be a addition to our young family. We both was kind of hoping for a girl, but that's what happens when things are not in our control. But our only hopes was to have a healthy baby, and we did.

On September 18, 1963, our second child arrived. Derrick K Harvey, six pounds nine ounces healthy and well. Mary was now becoming quite the mother, well me, I was the head dipper washer. The pamper age had not yet arrived but we now knew pretty much about this parenting.

I think about 2:30 p.m. Chicago time, the news flashed that President Kennedy had been shot. Sadness fell upon people everywhere. The suspect was Mr. Lee Harvey Oswald. It looked as if Mr. Kennedy was trying to do something about the conditions of the minorities in this country. Many good social programs came out of the Kennedy's administration. Some folks called him the black people's president, because what he was trying to accomplish did bring some relief to blacks, and all other deprived people. Because we were the ones who needed the most, that was a great help for the common people and some in my opinion wasn't that great. One was the urban renewal program, this was when the city would come in and demolish a entire community of people homes, and replace it with playgrounds, neighborhoods parks, swimming pools, which all of them was in minority communities. But most was bought on contract, and the home were just taken away, and it was nothing we could do but move. That's the way the American dream went for most of the minorities, and in most cases things hasn't changed.

Mr. J. Edgar Hoover, director of the federal bureau of investigation, was using every opportunity he could to defend the violent acts of the KKK. This man was the true picture of a Klansman himself. He hated the word civil rights, and his respect for Dr. King was about zero. I think his views for, then we were called Negro's, were less than that. With the Black Panther party growing and the civil rights movement in full steam, unlike the Klan the black panthers was providing after school programs for lower-income families, after school programs for children with difficulties with reading, math, and spelling. They formed soup kitchens, also helped seniors with paying their utilities bills, and many other benefits that were needed. But Mr. Hoover said, "This group must be stopped, because they weren't anything but militants, thugs, preparing to overthrow the government." But the Klan's were still doing their same things, and still is and they were only exercising their constitutional rights, but where was the protection of the rights of the victims?

These were some very difficult times in this country, but the thing was then and still is today in my opinion, could have been resolved just by having the laws enforced equally, which is still a very big concern of mine. And the illusion of freedom hasn't changed. The daily machine was working very well for what it was created for, and that was for control.

Chicago street gangs emerged in the 1960s when a youth group call the Black P-Stone Rangers developed into a criminal organization. The group's leaders, Jeff Fort, united the leaders of some 50 area street gangs into a single organization and called it the Black P-stone Nation. The group was controlled by a 2-man commission. They were called the "Main 21." The leaders called their group a socially self-help organization to help uplift their communities. And with this premise, they successfully obtained $1.4 million dollars in a federal anti-poverty funds. But these funds were used to support the group's illegal activities. A federal grand jury uncovered the mismanagement of funds, and Jeff Fort was sent to prison.

After Mr. Fort's imprisonment, the believed success of the Black P-Stone Nation resulted in the formation of many other street gangs, which was supposed to have been a motivation for social and political. But they became very disorganized. In the meantime, others became quite organized and very sophisticated. These groups were involved in prostitution, armed robbery, burglary, extortion, and drug sales. The main two gangs were the Black Disciples, led by Mr. David Barksdale, and the Gangster Disciples, led by Mr. Larry Hoover. They followed Mr. Fort's example and they unified their gangs, forming the Black Gangster Disciple Nation. In the 1970s, this combined Black P-Stone Nation and the Black Gangster Disciple Nation controlled the Chicago drug trade. Record will confirm that they became bitter rivals. Their rage and anger left the bloodiest gang war in Chicago's history powerful but not free. Gang violence had spread to all four areas of the city. The Latin Kings, Black Stone Rangers, Disciples, and others controlled virtually every section of the city. The most notorious of all were the Blackstone Rangers, this one Mr. Jeff Fort. It seemed to me, and maybe many others that gang was on the federal payroll, these people did what ever they wanted killing terrorizing community-having businesses paying protection fees, and the Chicago police was doing nothing to stop this nonsense. As long as it was black on black crime, that's what it was called, it was ok. And this is very difficult for me to say, but years later after they had completely destroyed the southeast side of Chicago, they killed a white police officer. That's when the FBI and all other agencies came in and did what should have been done long before.

Gangs are not a new thing, but my reason for even bringing this up is these problems do have some negative play in this freedom we think we have. The word "thug" dates back to India in the year 1200 AD. It refers to a gang of criminals. Thugs that roamed the country pillaged towns in their course. These thugs had their own symbols, hand signs, rituals and slang. In the United States, we grew up with tales of our own form of thugs like pirates and gangsters, therefore, gangs are undoubtedly not a new concept. But my question remains, why do they still continue? And how can we as a free people clam to be free living under so much open violence? Through studies shown in 1991 there were an estimate of 4,881 with 249,324 members, so these are some of the things that prevents us from being free. The entire nation was saying, "What's the point?" I saw what seemed like nation at what I called a time where the fear of a culture permeated the entire human system like never before. I thought it was freighting living in Georgia but that was not even near what was going on then, and it's still around now.

My wife and I went back to the drawing board, and October 5, 1964, we were blessed with our third child. Pechina S, Harvey, she now has two children of her own, but she still defends her position as our baby.

In 1964, Rev. Dr. Martin Luther king, Jr., was awarded the

Nobel Peace Prize. From 1964 to 1968, both triumph and trag-
edy were a part of the civil rights movement. When black Americans in the South tried to register and vote, white officials often
intimidated them. Blacks were forced to take "citizenship tests"
that white voters did not face. There was a nonviolent students'
committee that took on the task of helping blacks register to vote
in Mississippi. Students from the North went to help with this
project. That's the summer Andrew Goodman went South and
joined already civil rights workers Michael Schwerner and James
Chaney. They were beaten and shot to death by yes that same
group, the Ku Klux Klansmen. But it wasn't until 2005 that the
state of Mississippi convicted the ringleader. The Jessup County
in Mississippi is where the movie called Mississippi Burning was
based on and there are records of these kind of happenings in
other places in the South. But our constitution says yes, or is it
those who we call our elected official making sure these people
continue to practice the same criminal acts that they have been
doing for more than a century, leaving trails of black Americans'
blood in every state in this country? And I ask why?

On July 2, 1964, President Lyndon B. Johnson signed into
law the Civil Rights Act of 1964. He had tried hard to pass Kennedy's bill, which outlawed segregation in restaurants, hotels,
movie theaters, sports arenas, and other public places. This bill
also outlawed job discrimination on the basis of sex, race, religion, and national origin. Now check the United States constitution and see what it says; these things had already become law.
Then a year later, Mr. Johnson pushed through the congress the
Voting Rights Act of 1965, which assured black Americans their
right to vote. Now I need some clarification here; what happened with the constitution? And what good is it to the citizens

of this nation? Or should I say the black people? It seems like somebody's doing something very bad. Because everything they were supposed to have given us in 1964–5 had already been given in 1865. Why was this necessary in 1964–5?

The first part of 1965, the Southern Christian Leadership Conference started a voter-registration project in Selma, Alabama. Reverend Martin Luther King, Jr., and many other adults were arrested for marching, and many children were arrested in protest, too.

Then a group tried to march from Selma to Montgomery, the state capitol 54 miles away. And the welcoming committee, state troopers on horseback armed with their firearms, they used Billy clubs, bull whips, tear gas, and cattle prods to break up the marchers. But when the photos of the attack were shown on television, people black and white from all over the nation came by droves to Selma. On March 24, it was reported 4,000 protesters started a march to Montgomery, this time protected by the U.S. military. When they reached Montgomery five days later, on March 25, the number had grown to 25,000.

This freedom we've gained must have been bad from the beginning, but they still say we're one nation under God. Now they didn't say what god.

Then Muhammad Ali became the heavy-weight boxing champion of the world, but in 1964 he refused to fight in the Vietnam War. He was stripped of his title, but the Supreme Court ruled in 1974 that the government acted improperly. Ali regained his title after serving time in prison.

After many arrests, Martin L. King, Jr., realized true freedom could come with economic equality. He began a campaign for poor people, well I guess we know fell under that category.

And while he was in Memphis, Tennessee, supporting the garbage workers which was on strike, King was assassinated on the balcony of the motel where he was staying.

The war clouds of Vietnam were hanging heavy over the heads of all Americans, and in some ways, they are still there. General William Westmoreland was given the command.

"Black power," while winning gold and bronze medals, in the 1968 Olympic held in Mexico, black American athletes made names for themselves. During the medal presentation ceremony, Tommie Smith and John Carlos, gold and bronze medal winners in the 200m, raised a black-gloved fist and hung their heads when their country's national anthem was played. In doing this, they were protesting against racial segregation in the United States and were expelled from the Olympic village. Soon after, the clinched fist became a global symbol of brotherhood; what happened? But when the KKK raise their hands and salute, and recognize Hitler with the swastika, our laws protect their right to speech. This is their way our freedom is presented to us.

1968, the Democratic Party held their national convention in Chicago; this is probably one of the scandalizing events of the history of Chicago. August 26 to the 29, they were choosing a presidential candidate, but the different views over the war in Vietnam provided the fuel that flamed the fires between the Chicago police and the anti-Vietnam war protesters in the streets and parks. Riots like I had never seen before made me realize in this country, it's always a reason for separation but we keep repeating we're one nation, and I say divided into many pieces. We always say this or that caused a split, between our nations whether it's political, religious, gender, choice, or political correctness. We will find ways to cause that split, and the illusions continue, but we always see freedom. Well, if being free is living in constant chaos and confusion I guess we are, but to me, I chose harmony, togetherness, peace, and joy, which will produce prosperity and happiness.

Plowing our mules for so long I saw a animal weighing hundred of pounds, and very strong, but yet, being controlled by a seven year old child, simply because they had been condition to obey cretin commands. And it mattered not who gave the command they obeyed it, much like the people of this country. We've become so responsive to certain commands until we do just what the command suggests, we're always under a post hypnotic suggestion. When the hypnotist gives that right command we the subject react to whatever has been given while in a deep sleep or under spell. We're held captive by our fears, which are passed down from our past.

I've notice over the years how we have been lured in to a mind-shaping and controlling situation. During the cold war it was said, "the people of the soviet union was brain washed," but our system gave classes on that idea, and it has worked just right for the purpose of the party systems or groups, that's in charge at that particular time. And it matters not which one, because it's still the big ones keep eating the little ones, but very soon all the little ones will be eaten away. And then when that animal like behavior will become visible and that carnivorous instinct will kick in, and like the gray wolf of the north, they will began licking and the greed will over bear their science of understanding of what's happening. And they will consume themselves with their own powers, this is why I keep saying the picture of freedom we see it's nothing more than an illusion.

The rich and famous can't move out of their own little controlled group of rich people. The powerful in terms of education can exists only with the powerful. If you think of it, who are the most people school teachers know? Well yes, it's school teachers. Well, numbskull, you probably say, but the fact is when they aren't in school they never think of socializing with non teachers, lawyers, doctors, judges, policeperson, politicians, and name any others. And they all fit the same pattern, and they are afraid to walk outside of that circle, and afraid to let any other group in, so they assume they are free as long as they're within their own circle.

The human family is creatures of habit, and our habits keep us with our own kinds of creatures. I'm not trying to suggest everybody should always bunch together, but let it be by choice and not status, because the lines of our boundaries are drawn by our fears.

Throughout the early Sixties, this country suffered a major social, racial, economic, academic, religious, and political, separation, and the reuniting hasn't happened yet. I keep mentioning the fact of being humanly disconnected and some of the reasons we are so afraid of everything. It's simply because we have lost that connection. Just as a room with beautiful lamps, but if the electric cord has became disconnected from the outlet in the wall, then you know what the results will be. And what I've noticed over the last fifty odd years, how we have used different things to grab, and hold on to. I said earlier when we were on the farm, it seemed like we was always holding on to something, plow handles, hoe handles, ax handles, or something, it just seemed like it was always something we had to hold on to, and that hasn't changed. I believe it's just a part of this marketing system. We have given up on doing our own thinking; for the most part, we wait for the sales ad before we can do our shopping. Our daily activities are planned around the weather report. These things might not seem to be important, but the importance is we've given away our freedoms for what we now call convenience. I think we deserve all the convenience we want, but let's not return to the frog in the slow warming water situation. Putting a frog in cold water and slowly let it heat the frog will sit there and cook to death, and somehow it seems like we're headed down that same path. What freedom?

I will continue to try promoting the spirit of the American principle, and the spirit of freedom, by first practicing the loving thy neighbors, and becoming a better citizen through a freedom that can't be found in the constitution.

I started to realize the racial problems we were having had nothing to do with geography. Living on a farm near a small town in the South in the Forties was just a small part of a much larger problem that needed to be fixed, and I haven't seen any signs of change.

Now we've entered into another millennium, and I truly don't see any thing different, but the power of choice is still working.

Racial separation, racial injustice, and equalities are all shared by what this country calls its minorities groups, but racial separation is basically between the white citizens, and the black people, because the blacks are in a class of its own. And honestly, it doesn't look as it will ever change, unless we learn to change our way of thinking about this false freedom, and start learning how to live free. And the choice is within the individual, this is mine and I choose to live free yes, still in a not so free society. Oh they say it's different and things has changed, but I say, "it's the same thing just changed around."

We were parents now, and our children were growing up.

My concern was how could we teach love to this new generation of people? The gangs were recruiting our boys at a very early age, and this was another element that was completely new to us. The only gang I ever belonged to was a baseball team, but these thugs weren't any different than that KKK group. So the road to freedom has narrowed considerably, from the United States constitution to the survival of the fittest. I began to see how the respect for life and the quality of life or just life itself started to vanish, some how the same venom that once spud from the fangs of the Klan was now flowing from the fangs of our own kind. Where we once had to rely on each other for protection, now we had to beware of the same.

I believe my earlier years in the south gave me a better appreciation of my life today. The values our parents instilled in each of us enabled me to make that balance.

But there will always be struggles with racial injustice in America as far as blacks are concerned, but what am I going to do? I'm going to continue to use what was given to me some sixty odd years earlier. Love when it isn't in a pleasant situation, and help whenever the opportunity presents itself, not be discouraged if things doesn't happen right away, and don't wait for the next person to do what needs to be done. These are the pathways that leads to true freedom.

But what I find quite funny about this illusion of freedom is when we lived on the farm, the boundaries had already been laid for us. We knew exactly where every line had been drawn, but now the lines are drown in our minds. The first thing given was the American dream, as it's called, so they are telling us we can't even have a dream of our own. So the dream they gave was get a good education from the most famous college so you can brag about what school we attended. Then, there is always some place that will give you a position because of the school's reputation. Then you will be able to get the biggest house on the block and all of the credit cards, and they only give you the false feeling that you're better than everybody you know. But the truth is, we've just been had. You just lost the freedom of associating with old friends. Now you have to associate with just the ones who meet the status-quo, which all become quite comfortably, uncomfortable, with each other but you find your self trapped in a place of make belief, the very wealthy as do the very financially disenfranchised.

We all have our own boundaries that were made by someone other than us. I watch the Hollywood scene; they only have their own population they can feel free and relaxed with. If it's not someone wanting to interview them, it's that paparazzi group trying to find something bad to talk about, so they are not living free lives. So I ask, where can we find true freedom? I think true freedom is found in being able to reach beyond all racial, cultural, political, academic, economic, religious, social, affiliation, preference, and/or orientation and find that commonness of family hood, and re-join connect to the family. Again, it doesn't matter what school we might have attended or the type of business or career we might pursue. It isn't important how much stuff/things we might have; we're all just little tadpoles trying to become frogs.

Another things I noticed with the gangs was most of the members were young and not very well educated. They said they just wanted to belong and have some freedom, but they were just becoming truly controlled, just like the mobsters. Once the door opens and one enters, the door shuts behind you, and there is no way out.

It matters not where you are or who you may be; the lines of confinement are al ways there. But we are a free nation, with all of the liberties going for us. Well, I think different. We're all caught up in a huge web, in a world of make believe. I think back many years ago, we would find huge webs spun by spiders and the larvae of different insects. These webs could be found all over the place. They are very carefully formed by weaving. Sometimes you could find a entire cluster of bushes and small trees completely wrapped in these webs. When an insect and sometimes a sparrow gets caught, it's virtually impossible to escape, but this is for the purpose of survival and not control. But on the other hand, I see this human family in somewhat of the same situation, but the difference is, it's not for survival. It's purely for control.

Daddy told us the last thing you do, make that the best of all.

Now I realize he was teaching us a legacy then because the last thing you do will be most remembered. I think somewhere along the way, Easy Eddie learned how to live a free life. Freedom—is it a given right, or is it a matter of choice?

When we speak of freedom, do we mean freedom of the things our constitution speaks of, or do we mean the freedom that allows us to live a free life within the realms of the constitution itself? Because the way I see this thing we call freedom, it's more about the way we choose to live rather than the way we're forced to live.

There are countless stories about people living free, far beyond the realms of any kind of a assumed freedom that was given by a governmental powers, and in some cases there were absolute none, the same way we were in Georgia, but the difference is we were supposed to have all the freedom that our constitution allowed, but it wasn't available for us. But we were taught how to live a very good and free life, and that was by choice.

"Choose you this day whom ye will serve whether the gods which your fathers served that were on the other side of the flood, or the gods of the Amorites in whose land ye dwell; but as for me and my house, we will serve the Lord" (Joshua 24:15, KJV). The reason for this is to show why choice is so necessary in our growth. It matters not what we are involved in. The first thing we saw was, it's ok not to choose the same things or the same values, but you must make a choice. Life is all about choices, whether we realize it of not. Everything comes by choice, even if you think you're not making a choice. The results will show just what choices have been made, so I thank God today, Douglas, Kira, and Ethel, first made the choice of how they wanted us to overcome what could have easily been serving the gods which our forefathers served. On the other side of physical slavery, if those seeds had been sown in the soils of our minds, it would have produced the fruits of bitterness, and hatred, and that could have denied us our inalienable rights to live a complete free life.

Those are the choices they made, and that gave us the opportunity to experience the real meaning of freedom. We never thought about that false one that's offered by our constitution.

We now understand more about the power and the benefits in making good choices. We choose to love rather than hate; we choose to serve rather than being served. I know the quickest way to greatness is through service.

Being born in Georgia and living in other states, I am able to see quit clearly that living in the South wasn't the only place injustice was being practice. The poisonous venom of racial injustice fueled by hatred and prejudice against another because of color, I still have a real problem trying to understand the real reason for this. And what I see, it's basically between the white and black citizens, or white citizens and black people, because it seems if we're not a part of this citizen factor, we are just here.

I cannot believe more can't be done to fix this long-going problem in this country. I feel like the people who are calling the shots, those we elect in governmental affairs, have the same racist mentality as those a few hundred years ago. But the horrible truth about this is, the majority of the white citizens today see nothing wrong. What is even worse, a great deal of blacks says things have gotten much better over the last fifty or so years. I would like to know where, and in what way?

Living through the Forties, Fifties, Sixties, Seventies, Eighties, Nineties, and into the twenty-first century, I can truly say the more things change, the more they remain the same.

From 1946 to 1964, there were over 70 million babies born in the United States. Never before or since were so many babies born in such short period of time. These huge additions to the population were caught up at the very beginning. The baby product manufacturing companies prepared us for the next sixty or seventy years with new products that would be consumed on a daily basis, and showed us how we couldn't live without them. But we did pretty good before they came.

"Disposable" was the message they sent. Use it today and buy it again tomorrow. The diaper industry climbed to a record-breaking height, and the way it's done is always around convenience. Baby formulas came out of the woodwork. The traditional know-how of rearing children was no longer acceptable after years of successfully doing so.

From the 1930s thru the 1960s, babies didn't worry about the parents drinking alcohol/or smoking while carrying them. There were no fancy baby cribs covered with lead-based paints; no child-proof gadgets bottles and cabinets with locks. There were no helmets for riding bikes. We survived riding in our cars with being fastened down with seat restraints or air bags, which they have admitted that the air bags will cause harm. I'm still addressing this freedom we all have, we found great pleasure in riding in the back of our pick-ups drinking water right out of the faucets, water bottles? Maybe the garden hose, two or three friends shared the same soft drink, playing was enough exercise. Overweight was never a part of our lifestyles, we were not tied to a cell-phone every time we left home, and we played until dark without causing an amber alert what we did asked another child. We rode self-made bicycles down hills without breaks, learning a ditch and bushes was the best place to stop-um. Playstations, Nintendos, X-boxes, video games, no cable, no video movies, the only surround sounds was the out-doors and P-C or chat-rooms. We found our friends just by going outside, broken bones, cuts, bruises, teeth knocked out, and the only lawyer we knew was Perry Mason. My first gun was a BB I got for Christmas at five years old our parents always agreed with the law and made sure we obeyed it.

The last 50 or so years have produced some great inventors and different ideas. We had freedom, success and prosperity but not much responsibility. Yes, there were some failures, too, but we also learned how to deal with it.

We saw the whole baby industry rise to such economical level like never before. We also were taught we didn't need to do our own thinking anymore. We had the media and many different kinds of agencies to do our thinking.

Each year became more intense. The way we had shopped before was gone forever. The toy industry changed dramatically from the traditional cap pistol to more real like automatic weapons.

The social language changed to fit the marketing strategies. The education became more competitive to where we're going for the American dream in full speed. The concept was to go to the biggest university and graduate, get the highest paying job, buy the biggest house, get two cars, and get every credit card that was out there, and never be free from debt again. Now you are living the American dream.

By the time all of these seventy plus million captive audiences of consumers were up and running then came the all time hot-rod automobile, then the small compact. Now with all these people with so much spending power and their families growing, it was a necessity for that second car, another link in that chain then the mini-van and then the SUVs and yes, I'm right there too.

From 1946 to 1964, these boomers were entering college. By 1984, the last group was in college. The first group was ready for the work force. Everything was all lined up for the takeover. The first group was buying big houses, and they had every major credit card that was available. Now we are convinced the more credit cards we have, the more spending power we have. The bells of freedom are tolling. When the second group gets out of college and in the work place, the first group is almost ready to start thinking about that huge motor home.

You may ask why I am talking about all of this in this book. Well, I just want to show how different situations and circumstances often will seem so different, but the harsh reality is, there's no different between freed and enslaved. The only difference is in formal slavery, the chains were on our legs. Now they're fastened to our minds. It matters not where you are or what form of control; the fact of the matter is, we're still not free.

From 1955 to 1995, these are the mayor's elections to serve the city of Chicago. Richard Joseph Daley, elected April 20, 1955(died in office, December 20, 1976); farther to Richard Michael Daley, who is currently mayor.

After Mr. Daley died in 1976, his successor, Michael Anthony Bilandic, from December 28, 1976- April 16, 1979; Jane Margaret Byrne, April 16, 1979, April 29, 1983; Harold Washington, Chicago's first black mayor, April 29, 1983-November25, 1987(died in office); David Duvall Orr, November 25, 1987-December 2,1987 (8 days, interim); Eugene Sawyer, December 2, 1987-April 24, 1989 (acting, elected by city council); Richard Michael Daley April 24, 1989- present.

Between 1976 through 1989, there was a power struggle between the city council and the mayor's office, but somehow they survived.

Living in Chicago for so many years gave me the opportunity to see how such a racially diverse society living in so many confined boundary, and these lines were drown in the mines of all of us. Even though we were living as one very large city, each racial group kept their boundary's distance from the others, and that created a since of ownership or control of that particular area. Which caused another problem, which resulted in territorial control, which led to some kind of violence, so where was the freedom? There wasn't any.

I've noticed over the years how we, as a free people, have the need to always be attached to something. It made us feel more secure, or maybe just belonging, when slavery was said to be illegal. A great many of the slaves stayed with their present masters because of, one, fear. They feared leaving the only thing they knew, and leaving with nothing and nowhere to go. And two, they were afraid of facing the unknown. It's our nature to return to the past, return to what we know, we rather re-visit the past no matter how horrible it might have been, than by faith, challenge the feature, because it's a place we never been before. So we remain victims of our fears, and we still call this freedom.

We've come through the books catcher, large handbags, extra fanny packs, shopping bags, but the new wave is the backpack. First we saw, on the backs of our school children's, then in the last few years I've seen packs on the back of a great many of adults. It's like we feel alone without having something attached to us, and I believe it's because we have became so disconnected from each other, and these items gives us another false feeling of security. We are all fixed to the thought that we're better off without anyone outside our own personal circle, and that's mainly just the people we live with.

After living in a great city like Chicago for so long, and seen so many different races and cultures, of people co existing together but not living together, it becomes very clear, the reason again is fear. And I'm still wondering how we continue to claim freedom and living in some cases our entire lives in constant fear, and our fears are embedded so deep in the soils of our minds and souls. I would guess, the roots are so deeply planted, until they reaches back through many generations, and I think, it's highly unlikely most of us will ever really experience the true meaning of living free, what a shame.

What I would like to say now, having love as the foundation of our lives, it produced nine pretty good citizens which I would recommend to be anyone's neighbors.

Rosie Lee, born January 24, 1927 in Cunningham, Georgia divorced as we earlier said she was the first of nine of us. She moved to Youngstown, Ohio, married until she divorced her husband and moved with us in Chicago in 1953–54 her and her four children. She then joined the (ACD) program (Aid For Dependant Children) but that didn't last for long. She said she was not cut out for depending on the state to take care of her children. So she did different kinds of work house cleaning, factory work one place was the beginning of the popular artificial Christmas trees, they were just silver alumni, Kraft house trees was the name of the company. And anything else, because it wasn't much available for blacks, even less for black women's. Much later she was hired with the city of Chicago as a junior clerk and then a senior clerk in the water department.

She worked many years and retired as a supervisor in the department of sewers one of a very few black women's that had risen to that level, under the leadership of then commissioner Ed Quigley, who saw something about her that she could undertake the responsibilities of that position and she was very helpful to many people. I don't know, as does anyone ever know, what would have been. But it's certain that the outcome would not have been as well had she not taken the path that was laid out for us. She later moved to Florida to see after a cousin. After about ten years, she returned to Chicago, bought a house, and she remained there until her death on December 5, 1998.

Though each of us made our own decisions of choosing what we wanted to do in lives, we all kept the same focus on trying to become better Christians, better servants, better friends, and better neighbors. I think to some degree we've made it quite a success.

Sister Laura Ann, born august 23, 1930, was the second child. After leaving the position at the Chicago Bar Association, she had early attended and graduating from a very prominent cosmopolitan school, but her sight was still on a career in the fashion-modeling arena. But again, the doors had not opened for beautiful black women's, and after trying every thing she could to get in that profession, she settled in the textile industry. First as a switch board operator/store model, then being promoted to merchandise buyer, where she stayed until her early retirement, due to health complications in the eighties, until her death February 25th, 2002.

Ethel Lee (Gee) Harvey, born October 7, 1936. She worked beside daddy and Fred in the fields until I was old enough. Then I became the next one to do the plowing after moving to Chicago she was diagnosed with diabetes and this was some very tough times. But now we really knew how to go where the real solution was and that was in Jesus, by prayer, after so many trips to the hospital they finally had it under control. Now this sister had the pure heart of a natural servant, although she had very poor health most of her adult life. She never refused to extend a needed hand to anyone. Anywhere there was a need for service, you could always find her there. She worked as a seamstress for many years until her sight became bad, and then heart problems, but never that heart that belonged to the Lord. She kept that part very active, as a choir member for nearly forty years she served as president of the choir several times. After a long battle with various illnesses she was called home April 17, 1999. Her favorite song was "I'm committed," quite befitting for her.

Brother Eddie L. Harvey was born May 8, 1942. Ed and I had a very special relationship from the very beginning. I guess

I realized I had to play big brother as Fred had been to me but that's the way it was.

After growing up in Chicago, his teenage years were quite different from the rest of ours. He was kind of on the wild side. He took to the street life with gang involvement, but our prayers were always for him to realize the road he was taking was not at all what he had been taught. But it was to no avail until his late twenties. He went to school and became a machinist. He always had the hands on approach to making things, and that worked. But after awhile, with a failed first marriage and jobs closings, he went on a drinking spree. That landed him in a alcohol treatment center. I took him in and walked with him for the entire time I visited him every day, as his mentor no more than what he would have done for me or anyone else. After he dried out I suggested he change his environment, well he did and shortly after he moved to Memphis, Tennessee. And this is where he became a believer in Christ. Most of the time, we never find our way until we become lost. After a few years studying there, he moved back to Chicago and went to seminary school. He was ordained as a minister and later pastured a church, where he remained until he succumbed to a long battle with bone cancer and kidney failure.

Favorite scripture: "Trust in the Lord with all thine heart; and lean not unto thine own understanding. In all thy ways acknowledge him, and he shall direct thy path" (Proverbs 3: 5–6, KJV).

Born May 8, 1942 - Feb 17, 2003

Hardly a day passes when one or sometimes all of them don't cross my mind. But the pain of not having them around is nothing like the joy of the memories from the times we shared before, and the hope of being together again.

We learned quite early how holding on will keep you from moving on, but the memories can be the fuel that keeps the wheels turning. All you need to do is just keep moving in the right direction.

Sally Doris Roper, after finishing high school, married her first husband, Joseph Roper, Jr. Together they had three children: Pamela, Mark, and Joseph III. She began working at the United States Post Office as a mail handler. Then she worked her way up the ladder quite rapidly. She was appointed to a position as a union representative. After years of marriage that ended in divorce, she re-married Donald Earl Rice. She served in many levels through the union. Doris was always one that seemed to take steady hold of something and then set out to master it. After serving in many areas and turning down a very prestigious position within the manager's circle, she said her good-byes two years ago with thirty-five years of great service. You go, girl.

Helen Rose; now here's a real Christian soldier.

After she finished school, Helen's employment started at Craft House Trees with Rosie Lee. She made artificial Christmas trees. Then she went to Sara Lee. While working there, she started working in a doctor's office. She went to school to become a doctor's assistant. She too always had poor health, but she never stopped doing things for others. Then she had to leave the work force and go on disability. Always have worked in the church, and she sang in the choir. She is the chief editor of the church monthly newspaper. She also works with vacation Bible school. She now has an oxygen supply tank but seems like she is just getting started in serving other people.

Lillian Faye Mc Reynolds was the baby of the Harvey clan. After graduating from high school, she took a short tour in the

United States Air Force. She studied hematology, and after returning home, she married Ronald Mc Reynolds. Two children were born from that union: Evan and Loren. She started her career working in one of the local hospitals in the blood unit. After awhile and several promotions, she now is one of the department heads at Oak-forest hospital, which is run by the county board in the department of hematology.

We as a race of people were given another falsehood. See the reason I keep moaning and groaning about this illusion is, I'm sure this is the way they intend it to be, because I will not believe these lawmakers which we call our governmental officials, really can't see there's something badly wrong with the justice system in this country. And they're the ones that's breaking the law by not up-holding it.

From the 1950s through the 70s, there were many changes in this nation. Most or all were geared around the reformation of the black communities. From re-zoning, which was designed to keep the political power out of the control of black people, after being given our civil rights in 1964 they still had to keep the slave chains in place. Each time we move up a step, we find ourselves being pushed back ten. I'm still amazed how they keep changing things around just to serve the purpose at the time. We've been shifted around since the time of our arrival here, but never had a real place in the America's system, even as much as earning our place in the pages of the nation's history. Even though the blood of our people has stained the soils of every state in the country, and every business have used our labors to become very prosperous without just compensation, we've been denied equal opportunities in every area of human life. And we're not worthy of having a place in the American history, only a very few are mentions, our young people know hardly anything about the contribution that black Americans have made in the progress of this great nation.

Thanks to black history founder, Carter G. Woodson, who felt that it was necessary for black American to be recognized in our American history. He is the founder of black history. Why can't we just be included in history?

We have endured the pain of slavery. We are constantly denied the benefit of equal access to the law. We have been denied equal opportunities to the main stream of employment, especially in the corporation level, the television news, and the commercial industry is dominated by the pre- usual. And the list goes on to every area of life, but there is not a word of thanks for bearing the burdens for hundred's of years of free labor that helped bring this country where we are today. And I still say, this is my country, and I am an American, and I do have a place in this great and rich history of this nation, because of my parents, grand-parents, ancestors, and (grand-casters) if that's a real word, and myself. We've paid all dues might have been due to ensure my rightful place in the history books of our nation, but as I can't be given freedom, neither can it be taken away, and I will not allow anyone to remove me from the history of this nation.

Yes, I do observe February as Black History month, as do I observe the other eleven months.

The blood of black Americans has spilled on the soils of every state in this country, but for whatever reason, and we've not yet earned our place in our nation's history, so what I'm going to do? Just keep doing what I was taught years ago—keep living as a free American.

After doing a number of things in Chicago in the area of

service, my wife and I talked about moving but never really put forth any effort to make it happen. I was employed with Midwest Cargo, a local trucking company owned by Bob Cunningham. I was serving an account at Superior Coffee Co., located at 990 Supreme Dr. Bensenville, Illinois. This is a place I will never forget. I found relation with people that became my friends unlike any thing I had ever experienced. Jean Sajdack, Chuck Forester, Marge Stemick, Marilyn Wolke, Tim Whitecotton, Pat Kelly, Less Cole's, Danny Soti and so many more, but this bunch I worked directly with for so many years, these are some of the best years of my life. Then I started driving for R&R Transportation Inc. Roger Westland was a very free person and maybe just a little on the nutty side. I met Roger once he came to Superior on business, and he was hauling freight for them. After awhile, he asked me to do some part-time driving for him, and later I joined his team. And after a few years working with Roger and those entire Hi-Way cowboys.

After living in the Midwest for forty-five years and serving in numerous voluntary positions in various areas of life, which I found great pleasure in doing so. And the rewards has been most gratifying to say the least, so it's time for a change.

On October 1, 1995 we relocated to the greater northwest.

Living here has given me some of the most pleasant times of my entire life. We've gained many new friends, and we've allowed ourselves to be good friends to others. There's so much value in living a life of freedom, I've learned. By bringing this freedom to the table of life, it makes quality of living great, drowned from a good learning make the feast of the table of life more enjoyable.

I continued driving long haul for about two years after we moved. I got a job driving locally with Gresham Transfer Co. It is one of the oldest transportation company's here. I met some very fine people. I had driven quite a variety of trucks in the past, but this was much different. But receiving help from dispatch and other senior drivers, I was able to become quite well at doing the job.

I must mention, for record sakes, after leaving Mid-west Cargo every place I've worked, it was only two or three people, as they say "of color" around, but I was always treated well. But Daddy said years before, "People will treat you one or two ways: they'll treat you the way you act, or they will treat you the way you allow them to." I'm still trying to discover something I've learned on my own, because all I am is what my parents taught me. They gave me the ingredients and told me to live a life where people will respect you, first by respecting them. So far, so good.

It's very important to see how people are already in place to become a very significant part of our lives. When we moved, my wife became a licensed childcare provider. Her first was a neighbor in the complex where we lived. Soon after, through she received a call from a young lady about her new-born baby boy. Jennifer McCollum made an appointment with Mary and then agreed after a few more interviews. And she brought the baby, Taylor is his name, and his little brother AJ, Anthony. So this relationship was formed out of a need to help two people get to another point in their lives. Jennifer was a manager at a very famous fast food chains and we needed some extra income, and the outcome is, we helped raise AJ, and Taylor, and Jennifer, she's now an RN at one of the hospital, and they are doing very well.

After getting settled in at our new home, I was re-visited by my old passion—bowling. In 1998, after being away from the game for 30 years, first I learned how different things were. Equipment had changed dramatically. I was completely lost, but a good friend, and a excellent bowler, Charlie Tyler, took me under his wings and taught me the new rules. And already having a good foundation of the fundamental of the game didn't take much to get me back, with much practice I've became a pretty good bowler. Valley Lanes Bowling Center has become our second home. This is where most of our close friends are. My wife and I celebrated our 34th anniversary at the bowling center. These people were our first new friends, and now they're our oldest new friends. Terry Pierce and his lovely wife, Cathy, are the owners of the center. It personifies the meaning of family center. It's just like a big family of people having a great time.

Lisa Walck and John Pittenger are the managers. This is where our new friend base began, and it has grown to a very large family. I would love to mention every individual person because they deserve to be mentioned, but it's impossible, and I know I'll forget someone. But it is a bunch, and they all would understand and forgive me. After joining the Friday night mix-league, after a year or so, Lisa asked me, "Alton we need another coach for the junior's I would like you to help us out with that. Valley has already sent your name in and paid for the classes." So I became a certified coach level 11 and the bronze level USA Bowling Coaching certification which give me the chance to help some of our young people develop their skills in bowling. I also have two grandchildren; Beronsha, now 17 (SHA), and Brandi (Miss Bran), she's 10. Both bowl very well.

Again my calling, the city of Beaverton had a notice in the Your City, a every two month paper, needing volunteers for a position on different commission boards. So I submitted a application alone with my resume, and within a few weeks, I was called for an interview, our mayor, Rob Drake, and then the city council president, Forrest Soth, I'm happily serving my second term as a city commissioner, on the human rights advisory commission. Alone with my very good friends and colleagues, our (Chair) James Maguire, (Vic, Chair) Heminder Singh, (Staff Liaison) NicolleWynia-Eide, Susie Brothers, Marlin Hofer, Francisco Ravelo, Sierra Redwine, Nader Sabahi, and former commissioner Ann Bliss, serving with and learning from this group of individuals has truly been a blessing for me. We have a very diversified group with a large range of experiences from different points of view, and that gives us a very unique perspective on our decision making and we will seek equal justice for all whom we represent. And this has given me a greater commitment to the protection of our rights as human beings, and not limited to race, sex, color, origin, religion, preference, of choice, or any other affiliation. If any falls under the categories of human beings, those are the ones we are there for.

My friend, Rob Drake, has a great sense of humor. He always makes comments about me being from Chicago, meaning the Big Al era, but it's all in fun. He and his wife, Ellen, will receive the second copy of my book.

We as a nation have overcome some very trying times, while enjoying the benefits of prosperity in so many ways. We've dealt with wars, conflicts, seems like it was war activities in every part of the world, right or wrong, just or unjust, we were there. I've lived sixty years in one century, and six years in the new millennium. We closed out the 20th century with fears of Y-2-K, and what seemed to be, to some a complete new way of life as we once known it, not wanting to thank of what might happen. Well that fizzled out with no unusual events. Much wasted food, water, and many other survival products, with no place to use them. The people we elect to keep us informed told us "it would be a huge (glitch) in the computerized system." We've became so use to depending on, but nothing happened, and they never told us what went wrong or right, as always, it passed on without a word. Then in the second year of a brand new century came the biggest scare for the American people surely of my time, 9/11, 2001, when our eastern seaboard came under attack. Now this was the big one, and triggered of a new wave of fears, for this big bad free nation, they said terrorism has struck the United States. Well I thought it had been here a long time before and doing well, this one was on a bigger scale, but this one gave them, "meaning the great dim god's" of our nation, a chance to inject another dose of fear into the veins of our free society. And they even brought a measuring device with it this time. They wanted to snatch away another of those so call freedoms and liberties. They would change the color of the fear bar, from orange, to yellow, or red, and whatever they thought of, and we the people responded just as they thought, and like Y- 2- K, nothing happened. Now, how does this sound? We were told, "It's going to happen again. We don't know when, nor do we know where, but we do know it's going to happen. And next time it will be bigger than the last one." But each time they made sure they added, "Just be vigilant. Go out and do what you've always done, and don't worry." Now this doesn't sound like what these people we elect should be telling the people. The signs of freedom seems to be fading right before our eyes, don't they? It seems to me they were promising us, "We'll get you, just wait." When the time comes, all they have to say is, "We told you it would happen," and just like an escape artist, they are scot-free.

There was plenty of talk about anthrax found in various

places, which brought on another fear. Then there was talk about smallpox and the West Nile Virus. They talked about bridges being targeted. For awhile, every weekend was extra protection, they said. Then came the SARs virus, and the latest one is the bird flu. It's always a different scare tactic. I'm trying to put this freedom into another perspective, and the only thing I can see is that same ole illusion.

Get To Know Your Neighbors

(G 2 K Y N)

It's an idea that came to me after September 11, 2001. I think that day was the most horrifying day in the life of most of the American population. The attack was on a very small part of the soil of America, but the jolt was felt all around the world. I don't remember when the attack was on Pearl Harbor, but this one seems like it must have been somewhat different. I guess because so many innocent lives were taken. But after the devastating blow happened, one of the greatest country singers wrote and recorded a song titled "Where Were You When the World Stopped Turning?" Mr. Allan Jackson, this song, I think touched the very fabric of each of all our beings. And this song just kept playing inside my mind, over and over until it finally hit me. In that song he says, "Did you stand there in shock at the sight of that black smoke rising against the blue sky? Did you shout out in anger in fear for your neighbor or did you just sit down and cry?" Then it was very clear, just how this horrific event happened. The thought came; how could I fear for someone if I don't know him? Well, that's where the idea for G2kyn came from. And another place in the song, he mentioned "The greatest is love." My hope is to use this organization and re-build the fabric of a torn society, by one neighbor at a time, using that age-old principle call love. I believe this nation can be that nation of hope, the pathway to freedom, and start rejoicing in the spirit of liberty and justice not only for all, but to all.

I hope we as a people learn one most important lesson. Let's not wait for something to happen before we come together, but let's come together. When it does happen, we will already be tighter.

You are invited to visit us, and your comments are welcomed.

Here's a family I met at Valley Lanes. They're so unique and similar to my own in so many ways.

The Leidelmeyer's, René, his wife Gaye, Their four children Deborah, Jacqueline Almyra, Hedwig E. David L. and Audrey M. This is one of the first families we met after our moving to Oregon.

The first time we met was when we joined the Friday night bowling league. Their team was the first team we bowled against. Rene's team was his wife, Gaye, two daughters, Almyra (Mia) Hedwig (Heidi), and himself. It was a five-person team. I don't know who the other member was at that time.

The first thing I noticed was the friendlessness and love between them that brought a real balance in the family. They seemed always very happy, even when they might not have had a great night with their game, and that wasn't very often. Another thing that was quite apparent was how they expressed that warm and loving feeling among each other that transcended to others around them. After a few years of bowling with them, and in different state tournaments, we became good friends. We began sharing our life experiences between each other, and was I surprised at how our lives held some of the same difficulties in the earlier times. Rene was born March 26, 1930, in Java, Indonesia. In 1953, he married a very fine and beautiful young lady, Gaye Mundler. She was from the west of the island. Her parents owned a tea plantation, and her grandfather owned a chicken farm and sold eggs all around the island. This union was blessed with four children, which I've been blessed by knowing three of the four. Rene and his three brothers and one sister were born into a very affluent family lifestyle, as was his wife. His father worked for the railroad. They were always surrounded with servants and the luxury of not doing anything for him self. He was raised with very high moral values, his family was also Christians.

But Rene was somewhat of an outcast from his family because he found delight in associating with the servants. Now that was a no/no, but I see René was already learning how to live a free life. His father was very much involved with the game of soccer. His father's team had shoes uniforms and the hole shooting match, but René had a plan. He wanted his team, which was made up of the servants and himself. He asked his father to buy his team their own uniforms. After negotiations, his father agreed, only if René's team could beat his team in what was a pretty big game; I suppose something like a playoff final. I can surely relate to this one. I can see his father's team all dressed in newly clean uniforms with soccer shoes looking like real professional. René's team probably really looked like they didn't belong with these guys, but don't focus on the looks. Well, Rene's team did get their uniforms.

It was during World War II, in a place best known for lost, when René didn't know anything about working because that wasn't a part of his early life. But he got his first glimpse at the ancient Japanese art of judo. He was 12, years old, and the Japanese soldiers had occupied his home the island of java in Indonesia, and splintered Dutch families like his into separated work camps, for men, women and children, and boys age 12 and older. He and the other boys were frightened of the soldiers, and the language barrier didn't help. But he was intrigued by their evening judo practices. After a while, the soldiers invited them to join in. Soon they were acting more like fathers and big brothers than the enemy. And when his skills far eclipsed those bigger boys, the soldiers rewarded him with an extra ration of rice. Talk about going from trials to triumph; this is a classic example of what can happen when you are carrying the torch of freedom that gives a light from within. It will give light to ways you never knew of.

René doesn't like his mind to linger there, but those years are a window into why he's made such of a connection with so many different people today. His passion is the art of judo, which he learned from his captors. It has aided him at some very pivotal moments in his life, and having the pleasure of sharing some of his earlier life experiences with me, that certainly has been a great joy.

He told me about the times during his detention, living in conditions that only could be understood if you were there. The living quarters were nothing more than an open building with no privacy at all. The flooring was dirt. Sometimes the room temperature reached 120 degrees, and the stench from human waste was just a part of the treatment. Now I can't understand what part of the human mindset causes another human been to treat another human beans this way, and there are places where this is still going on today. He told me how they went without food for many days at a time.

René either knew the advantage of living a free life, or he most certainly learned how to live free, because I know for sure he is a free man.

René married Gaye Mundler in 1953. Gaye's background is somewhat similar, but maybe not as atrocious, but none the less bad. She told me with a real big smile across her face, "Alton, I remember, when the Japanese soldiers were coming, my sister and I would run as fast as we could and hide under the tea bushes until they left." Now that's it's over she seemed quite relieved in telling these past but troublesome times. I did ask her, and I also reminded her I wasn't interested in any graphic descriptions, of her thoughts about what would have possibly happened if they had been found by the soldiers? She said "Alton, I don't know."

Her parents owned a tea plantation in West Java. Afterward her father worked as a slave on the bridge over the River Kwai, where he lost his life. Her grandfather had a chicken farm and sold eggs all over the island.

René and Gaye have four children. I think we met them by names earlier. They left for Europe when the second child (Mia) was four months. They left on an Italian ship to Milan, Italy, with two daughters, Deborah, Jacqueline Almyra, (Mia) which were born in West Java. From there they transferred on a train to the Netherlands, where the third and fourth children were born Hedwig E, and David L., and they lived there for five years. They lived in the southern part of the country on the border of the Netherlands and Belgium. They moved to San Jose in 1961 where the last child was born, Audrey M. They lived there until they moved to Oregon in 1963. There's so much about this family until it would take another book for you to really get to know the outstanding family, and who knows, maybe that isn't a bad idea. René has used those years as a window, and he's made a connection with the American Mexican children of farm workers who live at the Reedville apartments in Aloha Oregon. So what he learned from his one time captures, judo came to his aid at some pivotal moments, so the teacher wants to offer it to children whose parents work long hours but can't afford the recreational activities that often booster children's self-confidence. And he has passed the ancient art of judo to many young people, where he resides.

Relocating to another neighborhood takes some getting use to, but coming to another part of the country was a bit much to say the least. Learning to live in a different time zone, culture and a different way of life from what we had for the last forty-five years, but the adjustments wasn't that difficult.

Building a new friendship base came quite easy for me. The best place to start is right where you are, and that's what we did. As I learned a new system, everything I had done for the last forty-five years seemed a little odd at the beginning. But thanks to my new Oregonian friends and neighbors, it all came together pretty well.

I finished my driving career at Malarkey Roofing Products. This company has provided jobs for a lot of people for a long time. I'm very happy that the path of my life crossed at this place. It's been a real blessing for me. I found such joy in so many good friends such as I never had before. We never know where life's journey will take us, but I always try to prepare for the best so when I get there, I can enjoy it. My stay here has truly been worth the trip where you will find a friend, but if you are open to the opportunity that friend will find you.

One of the people I met and I call a friend, is Mr. Michael

O'Neal Malarkey. He's a man of great strengths, and very warm, and caring in all areas. He's a man that cares a great deal for the people working with him at the company in every level of employment, from the high-ranking person in management to the people working in production. He's a man with very few words, but he has great compassion for all. If anyone of the working family is in need for his attention, he doesn't just send somebody. He go himself; he and his dog, Zena. Mike has occasional cookouts at the plant. You will always find him under the tent. He cooks all the prime rib you could ever consume, and he does the serving himself—the true mark of a servant. It's been said, "Greatness is found in serving," and he truly is a great man in my eyesight. To evaluate his worth in service, he would outrank most.

But the person that keeps the wheels of the organization greased and turning is Ms. Mary Jane Murray. She seems to have the unique quality of helping solve most occurrences. Jane and her son, Ron and his wife, Gail, our families have shared some great moments at dinners and sit-down gatherings. These time I will never forget. We've found another extension in our lives, her son Ron is quite brilliant person and a very influential businessperson. When I need to know about most anything, if I can ever catch him, I always feel confident with his advise. Jane has worked there since 1948, and she's still as bossy as ever. I don't think it will ever stop, and that's a good thing. Shannon Yagi, we bowl/coach together at valley Jim Fagan, these are just a few of the corporate people that always made me feel like one of the team.

There are so many I've became very friendly with: Harry, Lynn, Larry, Bob, Jeff, Dennis, Willie, Paul, and all of my friends, most of whom I don't even know their names, but that's ok, too. Most of the time I refer to them as "brother," and I mean it.

There are four truck drivers who supply the plant with two products that complete the production of the roofing materials asphalt and limestone flour. Jim Lewis is lead Driver, one of his responsibilities is to order the asphalt according to production need's, and he drive as well. Ron Rider is another driver. He, Jim, and Frank, they are dual, meaning they haul asphalt and lime flour. I only do just one thing at a time.

One of the blessed things that could have ever happened for me was having the opportunity to meet which has become one of my best friends ever, Brother Frank, and his lovely wife Barbara Metcalf. Our friendship had an unusual beginning, but both of us realized it was a very special, spiritual meaning. Frank introduced me to another group of very fine people at North Community Baptist Church, which became my church family. The pastor at the time was Jeff Heart, and the friendship between Frank and Robert Bauer, the bond between the three of us has truly grown stronger, and more meaningful over the last six or seven years. And I see nothing can prevent it from becoming something even more special.

My specific responsibility was hauling lime flour from Ash Grove Lime Co., and I've made some lifetime friends there also; there's Brad, Jeff, Don, Criss, Steve, Shawn, and many others. Hugh, and all whom I don't know their names but so many great friends and so many great memories.

As I begin the conclusion of this journey, it's been a great pleasure and a new experience for me. Those of you that know me personally, I hope this book will bring us even closer. Those of you who never met me, I hope this book will form a mental link between us, that you might meet me through these pages. We all know, when we start a journey we never know what we will discover from the time we began until the time we end it. I've travel through 48 states and met many peoples, and now knowing how to live free, has truly been a blessing for me. And being able to enjoy a friendly relationship with all of my fellowmen without laboring under the burden of bigotry, prejudiced towards any people, or nay person, regardless of race, creed, color, gender, size, height, preference, or choices. I've learned to see people as my next of kin without any agenda. This way, I continue to enjoy the benefits of living free. In my community, the ethnic makeup has a wide variety of people, and there are no signs of racism. . These are my family, friends, and neighbors. Mr. Chang and Lee Park are my next-door neighbors. They are originally from South Korea, but nobody knows that because they're just my neighbors and friends. Mr. Park and I first started our get-to-know-your-neighbor community potluck picnic in July 2002. It has grown from a couple of houses to the joining city, which is Tigard. Last year well over one hundred neighbors attended, and we're expecting many more this year.

Ms. Ruth was one of the first to move in to our community. She is a very dear lady. Another very fine family that's very unique is the Larki family from Persia, Iran. They are super neighbors and friends.

We have a Bible study group comprised of five couples: Joel and Teresa Overland, Don and Pam Evens, Jim and Terri Mattila, Greg and Judy Martin. Joel and Teresa live three houses from us and they are two of the best friends we could have. Joel is the executive director of St. Andrews Legal Clinic. I am also a member of the board of directors of that very needed service. We are all very closely connected, and I'm very blessed to have friends and neighbor such as I do. I thank God for blessing my life with such fine people as he has. I must mention the fact that just a very few of my friends are people of my race, and it's not because I made that choice. The choosing wasn't mine, and I wouldn't have it any other way. If I had not been taught to live free and love everyone without reason, I would have denied myself of the inalienable right of living a complete, free life. I would have missed the opportunity to enjoy a great relationship with such wonderful people and so many great friends.

I'm sure we all at some point in our lives have said, if I could start over again, what I would do differently? Well, I believe most of us would maybe make some changes. Some would say I probably wouldn't change a thing, and you will find me among that group. My life up to this point has been nothing shorter than amazing, and the reason for that is because I've known the truth; and in that, I've been made free.

The things that keep us from being free are the things that don't expose the truths about them, or ourselves, so we remain in the darkness of our past. I believe one of the real reasons we are always ready to revisit our pasts is because we are trying to find a way out. I believe these are the things that keep us from grow- ing beyond our enslavements. So, in summary, I can say, there's absolutely nothing I would change in my life, because I am free of the past, and the paths I could have taken, but I maintain the course that was set by my parents which has brought me to where I am today. And do I recommend, this way is a good one? Absolutely. So when you start to look at anyone in a way that doesn't somehow reflect yourself, then I say take another look. When you see yourself in another person, you're seeing things as you should. But if we can't see ourselves in some form, maybe we need to take another look. We're all the same people, and to pretend we are something other than related is just another reason to continue to believe something that's completely false. To deny the truth is to live in pain, and the pain is not knowing the truth. Oh, I realize it's not so easy for us to see ourselves the same as someone else, especially if it's not our own color or social status, but that doesn't change the facts. Daddy told us that the best way to deal with our problems is to find the very nature of them; then we would know how to start to resolve them. To cut the tree from the top will not kill the root, because the tree itself is just an extension of the root and it will never grow out of the need of the root. And if remain rooted in the human family all of our differences are found within that rooted situation. And I see how we, or our elected official seems to over look that remedy, in solving the problems of our country. And we've given the government, as we call it, "the right to tell us how we should work, thank, raise our children, what foods we should eat, and where we should live." But none of these things they say really help solve the problems, but we still do exactly what we're told.

When they told us some thirty years ago we had to have seat belts in our automobiles, which in theory wasn't such a bad idea. But if your car was older than seems to me like 1975, you didn't have to have one, and the installment was optional. So my question then and still is: why weren't the lives of the people driving older cars important? Then came the air-bag systems. Now what reason would these devices be mandatory when they tell you they are dangerous if deployed, and that's why they were installed? This kind of freedom has a ring of deceit. I know someone will suggest that if I see so much wrong with the way this country's system works, why stay? And that's ok, too; I just see things quite differently from what is supposed to be. And I still ask, are we a free people, or is the freedom we see just an illusion?

Now, as I come to the closure of this conversation, I must say it's been a joy sharing my story with you. I hope you will find something that might be interesting and maybe helpful. But for now, I'll continue to let love be my guide.

"Thou Wilt Keep him in perfect peace, whose mind is stayed on thee, because he trusteth in thee" (Isaiah 26:3, KJV).

> Now; when my last deed
> Is done, when my last song has
> Been sung, then; will I take my flight
> Far beyond the sun, where I'll be
> Greeted by the Son, and he will say
> Servant, well done Amen
> Alton Harvey, Sr. 2006